CHRISTOPHER PRATT

Texts by David P. Silcox and Meriké Weiler

Prentice-Hall Canada Inc.

A Key Porter Book

ISBN 0-13-133645-2

Canadian Cataloguing in Publication Data
Silcox, David P., 1937-
    Christopher Pratt
Includes index.
ISBN 0-13-133645-2
1. Pratt, Christopher, 1935-   I. Weiler, Meriké.
II. Title.
ND249.P73S52   759.11   C82-094406-8

Published in Canada by:
Prentice-Hall Canada Inc.,
1870 Birchmount Road,
Scarborough, Ontario M1P 2J7

Produced by:
Key Porter Books,
59 Front Street East
Toronto, Ontario M5E 1B3

Designed by Ken Rodmell.
Composition by Canadian Composition Limited.
Colour Separations by Herzig Somerville Limited and Prolith Inc.
Printed by Ashton-Potter Limited on 200M Warrenflo Gloss.
Bound by Publishers Book Bindery, Inc.

Quotations which appear with the reproductions in this book are
the words of Christopher Pratt as spoken to Meriké Weiler and
David P. Silcox, and to Catherine Williams in an interview for
CJRT-FM Toronto.

Printed in Canada.
Bound in the United States of America.

For my mother and in memory of my father

NOW THAT THE LIGHT IS OUT

Now that the light is out
that made my windows
mirrors of my rooms,
and drew
strange insects from the darkness
to my house —
I can at last see out
into the black
and crowded night.

Christopher Pratt

Me and Bride
1977/80
Oil on board
44½″ x 107½″
Private Collection

CONTENTS

Studies for Night Window
1971
Graphite on paper
9" x 6"
Collection the Artist

I am looking out the window into blackness, seeing the reflection of the fireplace in the dark basement flat where I lived as a child. The notion of a night window, a window as a mirror, intrigues me because it is almost a perversion, a philosophical corruption of the idea of a window.

Night Window
1971
Oil on board
45½″ x 29¾″
Collection York University
Toronto, Ontario

Self Portrait
1968
Ink on gesso wash
8″ x 4″
Collection Mary Pratt

NIGHT WINDOW

David P. Silcox

EVERY WORK OF ART IS ORPHANED, sooner or later, by the time and context in which it was created. Christopher Pratt's works, I have no doubt, will withstand scrutiny in the future without the support of art criticism or individual reminiscences. All the same, personal information about creative people is often instructive and contemporary clues about their work helpful.

I first became aware of Pratt's work in 1964 but did not meet him until three years later. In 1969, I invited him to travel across Canada with me for several weeks as a member of a Canada Council jury. Since then, I have visited him in Newfoundland for a week or more nearly every year. Together we have driven the length and breadth of Newfoundland half a dozen times, sailed twice to Labrador, circumnavigated the Avalon Peninsula by sailboat and by car, and piloted our way from Nova Scotia across the great arc of the ocean to safe harbour in Newfoundland. I have come to know the man through his work and the work through the man so inextricably that I am now incapable of separating the two cleanly.

The relationship between Pratt and his work was puzzling and equivocal to me when I first knew him and has become more so over the years. In many ways the surfaces of the works are a perfect reflection of the man: intelligent, concise, reserved, and assured. In other ways the works' interior structures divulge what Pratt often appears to be: emotional, unpredictable, sensual, and uncertain.

Sharp contrasts and contradictions abound in his life and permeate his art. Some images seem to recall the past but stand as fresh and bright as new timber. The female figures that populate Pratt's work are virginal but also arouse the senses. Some pictures seem to be urging the viewer to accept a point of view, yet their cool neutrality can be interpreted as detachment. An enigmatic, suspenseful quality hovers over many works, but a sense of permanence is also felt. Certain aspects of Pratt's environment, background, and personality elucidate some of these contradictions and prepare for a discussion of his paintings.

The first noticeable contrast is the descent from the

windy, water-pocked barrenlands just south of St. John's, Newfoundland, to the wooded Salmonier River valley on St. Mary's Bay, where the Pratt house sits comfortably between road and river at the foot of a broad pond. The generous stretch of lawn, a rarity in the area, is fringed with flower beds and punctuated by trees and by a massive clump of rhododendrons. Across the Salmonier, stretching up and down the stream as far as the eye can see, is a primeval forest, or so it seems with its tenacious spruce and grey birch skeletons draped with immemorial lichens locally called old man's beard. Less than a stone's throw from telephone, television, and the other accoutrements of a modern home are lynx, moose, caribou, otter, and, in season, the redoubtable Atlantic salmon, finning its way back up to its birthplace. The river, here at the top of the tide, between salt water and fresh, contradicts itself: first the pond empties into the river, then the river empties into the pond. Visitors, sipping tea in the Pratt living room, may suddenly sense that the view has turned back to front or that they are watching in a mirror.

The house is an unpretentious, one-storey, white clapboard affair, originally a commodious summer cottage, which has been expanded in various ways over the past decade to accommodate four growing children, now beginning to leave home. Inside, the furniture and fixtures, in some cases ordered by catalogue, comprise an eclectic and practical style. Pictures by Pratt and his wife Mary and a few other artists hang throughout the house, and a Botticelli tondo in reproduction presides over the fireplace. In a corner of the living room is a piano on which Pratt sometimes amuses himself, and a wide range of music is available on record and cassette. Several floor-to-ceiling shelves of books bespeak a well-read family, and Pratt himself writes poetry, a literary bent that directly informs his work as a painter.

The animating force of this setting is the members of the Pratt family, from whom the Pratt I know is inseparable. There is a steady current of mostly cheerful, sometimes contentious, banter, as encouragement is given, guidance offered, plans discussed. Mary Pratt's common sense, care, sensitivity, and composure bring a scheduled order to what could easily become rambunctious disorder, for each of the children is determined and strong-willed. Her energy and control are surpassed only by Pratt himself, a restless, alert source of tyrannical energy. As a father, Pratt is like a stern, Old-Testament prophet as he commands, provokes, barks, cajoles, and teases. His gruff manner quickly dissolves in a moment of crisis, slight or major.

Mary Pratt is an accomplished painter who has picked up and set down her brushes many times between the demands of raising a family and providing steady support for her husband. She was already in art school when she met Pratt and before he decided to pursue his career as a painter. Her unswerving belief in his abilities steered him through the first few difficult years, though living with him is, in her description, like walking a tightrope.

She has been his regular and faithful critic, even though she claims to like all of his work so much that her opinion is not worth a great deal. Like Pratt, she is a fiercely independent thinker, and she is probably more influential than either of them cares to admit. Each is, paradoxically, more dependent upon the other than any other two self-contained people I know. Their intense relationship is the mainspring of the household and of their individual art. I never enter their home without feeling a palpable sensuality, a welling up of life in all its fullness and complexity, of life lived through the mind, the emotions, and the senses. Beneath the decorum, sobriety, and reserve, this sentience grazes the skin.

Pratt's Newfoundland ancestry spans three centuries and many generations. In Pratt's opinion, the maternal or Dawe side of his family, which came originally from Devon in the seventeenth century, accounts for much of his artistic temperament. His grandfather, William Dawe, a sea captain and merchant, was the self-trained architect of the wooden cathedral in Bay Roberts on Conception Bay, an imposing and imaginative building, which deftly marries European models with a long tradition of vernacular architecture in Newfoundland and Labrador. Pratt's mother had painted in watercolour as a student at finishing school. Some of her work hung in the house when Pratt was growing up, and she encouraged him in such pursuits as making Christmas decorations. In fact, the first art experience he remembers is painting water-colour Christmas cards with her. Most of his cards showed houses caught in the cold vice of winter.

The name 'Pratt' arrived relatively late, in the 1870s, with the Reverend John, hot from the forge of Wesleyan Methodism in Yorkshire. On the Pratt side, his great-aunt Charlotte did paintings that were highly prized by her parents, though her father disliked her fixation on winter landscapes. The poet E. J. Pratt, a great-uncle, and the acknowledged if unofficial poet laureate of Canada by the time Pratt was born, legitimized the idea that being an

artist was not a blot on the family escutcheon.

But more importantly, Pratt's paternal grandfather, James, a businessman, became a serious amateur painter late in his life. While Pratt was still quite young, James gave him Adolf Dehn's book *Water Color Painting*, an American primer illustrated with works by John Marin, Charles Burchfield, Reginald Marsh, and Edward Hopper, and another book, now lost, of work by Charles Sheeler, Winslow Homer, and Rockwell Kent. In his house, James Pratt maintained a studio, the first that Pratt saw. He was a convincing example that painting could be a manly pursuit.

The elegance and assurance of Pratt's paintings may stem from a desire to purify, but equally these qualities emerge from his ancestry and the history of the terrain in which he has enveloped himself. The raw geography of Newfoundland may imply a barbarous, rural society, but the truth is that many outport communities were once sophisticated, well-to-do, stratified, and elaborately organized. Turn-of-the-century sepia photographs, for example, which are among Pratt's cherished memorabilia, depict ladies in long gowns taking tea while the gentlemen, in full whites, play cricket on the green at Bay Roberts or Harbour Grace. The grand houses of these world traders were stocked with provender from Liverpool and London, Boston and New York, Naples and Marseilles, and the restorative pleasures of Bermuda and the Caribbean were enjoyed by their families decades before most Canadians could afford such holidays. A tradition of gentility, with accompaniments of servants, social occasions, and pro-scribed behaviour, was well developed in outport life.

Pratt's paintings try to capture the order and pride the little outports once boasted. He does not lament the economic changes that have occurred, for he accepts, with alacrity and understanding, the imperatives of modern business. What bothers him is the loss of a social order, of a cohesive hierarchy among men, where one's place is known and acknowledged and where a craft or a skill confers worth and dignity.

Pratt is a hereditary and a natural aristocrat in Newfoundland society, a man respected for his wisdom as much as for his accomplishment, for his firm regional commitment as much as for the recognition he receives outside the province. For generations the Dawes were part of the outport, mercantile aristocracy of the island society. In the twentieth century, several Pratts have distinguished themselves in business in urban St. John's. It is not surprising that Pratt naturally and easily assumes a sense of place, position, and responsibility, of *noblesse oblige*, both as a 'townie' and as a 'bayman.'

His popularity is not merely a result of artistic reputation, his honorary degrees, his sailboat's winning ways, or his political activities. His house is like the local manse, a partial mystery treated with cagey respect by the community. Most people, young and old, call him Mister Pratt. Visitors to his home often do not look at his paintings except out of courtesy or curiosity. They come, instead, to draw on the energy and sense of pride and integrity that emanates from the Pratt household, and chiefly from Pratt himself.

An example of Pratt's deep concern for pride, justice, efficiency, and tradition was revealed one day when we were sitting at anchor in the little harbour of Quirpon all through a long, hot, summer day in 1972, waiting for the wind to abate and allow our passage across the Strait of Belle Isle to Labrador. Early in the morning a large load of cod was forked from a long liner onto the dock nearby. By the time a truck from a distant fish plant came in the evening to haul it away, Pratt was beside himself with disgust.

While the cod baked on the dock, with no one caring enough to spread a tarpaulin or throw an occasional bucket of water over them, Pratt recited an indictment of political and social leaders who had persuaded capable men to burn their boats, join Canada and the twentieth century, and move to the city for welfare support. He was incensed that any system should deprive men of their pride of work or extract their last vestiges of shame. He decried the moral vacuum that had been created in recent years, and lamented the debasement of the fishery, not just its loss of traditional standards and values, but its seeming inability to modernize with energy, resourcefulness, and astute planning. Pratt was ashamed of the lack of leadership, and if he were not an artist he might well be a politician, for he sees both professions as capable of fortifying or restoring human dignity.

From time to time Pratt has become engrossed in politics, a pursuit he enjoys greatly and one that is never far from his mind. He has acted as campaign manager, canvasser, front-man and fund-raiser, and has confessed readily to the personal excitement he gets from public speaking. Running for elected office has been a serious temptation. Politicians, of both parties, are frequent visitors to his home.

*   *   *

To enter Pratt's studio is to enter a world as orderly as the past he knows and as neat as a Van Eyck painting. Every tool and accessory has its appointed place, working spaces are uncluttered, and the carpet, for a painter's studio, is spotless. He is not fastidious, for his car is usually a mess, but he is consciously organized and deliberate about those matters that he takes seriously. In his thought and speech, as in his art, he strives for clarity and order to a degree that often makes him appear dogmatic, conservative, and imperiously self-confident. These traits do sometimes apply, but the other side of the truth is that Pratt is open-minded to a rare degree, anxious to absorb new ideas, and extremely tolerant of contrary opinion.

For one so conservatively educated and so committed to traditional artistic methods, he is a surprisingly radical advocate of reform in human institutions and pro-grammes. As for his stiff self-confidence, it shields a fluttering indecision. He is always sceptical of his accomplishments and doubtful if anyone will like his work or buy it. His authority can dissipate in an instant: as he was finishing work on *Clothesline* (page 59), a local lad, who had come by about something else, called it 'a line of diapers.' After nearly four months' toil, Pratt caved in totally at the slight and would have destroyed the whole edition had his wife not prevailed and preserved a few copies. The experience made him leery of showing work in progress to anyone.

Like other vulnerable people, Pratt protects himself. His self-portrait of 1961, a graduation exercise at Mount Allison University, already shows him in a classic, defensive position, back to the window, arms crossed in what body-language experts say is the 'I don't want to reveal anything to you' pose. He looks severe and, at twenty-six, has lost much of his hair. The eyes of the window behind him are half-curtained, and it is winter outside. Pratt stares straight at the viewer like a cat; so do his paintings.

In conversation Pratt's crisply logical manner is also protective, but there are times when one can almost see his emotions bunched on the outer edge of his control like thoroughbreds at the starting gate. Though not sanctimo-nious about the habits of others, Pratt is a teetotaller; alcohol has been the nemesis of several relatives, enough to make him guard against the grip that addiction can have on the mind. Chiefly, however, he deflects all potentially serious or prying enquiries by keeping them on a taut surface of conscious exchange, where they skip out of sight, or by meeting them with a barrage of humour. He is one of the funniest and wittiest men I know, an inveterate ham, a captivating story-teller, kindly to those he satirizes, and not above pointing a moral. But when the inner man is revealed, one wonders if he will immobilize himself with the gravity of his own thoughts.

Pratt has three areas of serious concentration: fishing, sailing, and painting. Fishing was Pratt's first hobby-cum-profession, for he developed a passion and proficiency for it while he was still a boy trouting with chums in the brooks and ponds near St. John's where he grew up. Then came the more complex skills required in catching the wily salmon. From his yard, he angles for salmon where they rest before entering the pond, and he often rises and hooks them after others have tried in vain.

Typically, Pratt's forms of relaxation require a high

pitch of concentration, expertise, and knowledge. He loves to analyze a complex stream like the one at Trepassey, showing where the salmon will lie, suggesting what flies they will rise to and when they can best be pursued. His accuracy with a flyrod is uncanny, and he can see into the water like an osprey. On the Cloud River in northern Newfoundland, I have seen him stalking a salmon like an Eskimo after a seal, patient, tense, poised, wholly absorbed as he danced the fly back and forth until the mirrored surface of the stream was shattered by the sudden and terrific eruption of the king of fish.

Sailing for Pratt is almost genetically ordained. His great-great-grandfather on the Pratt side was Captain William Knight, one of the legendary sailors of his day, who piloted the American painter Frederick Church on his historic circuit of Newfoundland and Labrador in 1858. The Dawe family were sailors and merchants and, until a few years ago, made an annual summer pilgrimage to Labrador as their forebears had done for so many years for business, trade, fish, or seals. The migratory urge still bubbles to the surface in Pratt's plans from time to time. The ritual of the years leaves a durable trace.

Pratt approaches the business of sailing with the single-mindedness of the returning salmon. For most of his adult life he has had some sort of sailboat, but when, in 1973, he bought one of the world's finest and fastest racers, a thirty-foot, Canadian-made C&C, he had found another consuming passion. In rapid succession Pratt traded up through three C&C boats, *Walrus Too*, *Lynx*, and *Proud Mary*, until he ended up at this writing with the forty-three-foot *Dry Fly*. In it he has begun to

challenge some of the most difficult waters in North America, where heavy winds, dangerous currents, and rapidly changing weather are daily fare and where the bitterly cold water makes falling overboard almost certain death.

About these boats, his floating studios, Pratt has been endlessly fussy, not just because his life and his crew's depend on it, compelling reason though that is, but because aboard them he functions as he does in his studio. Sailing a sophisticated machine across the surface of the ocean requires absolute concentration. Pratt is relentless and unremitting in his pursuit of the maximum or perfect performance, as he adjusts shackles, sheets, weight distribution, and sails.

As an artist, Pratt's development has been affected by his sailing in crucial ways. Prints such as *Lake Ontario* and *Above Montreal* (pages 137, 158) had their genesis while Pratt sailed down to the Gulf of St. Lawrence from Toronto. *New Boat* and *Ocean Racer* (pages 133, 119) are based on general ideas about boats and, like other works, come from familiarity and reflection. Further, the subtleties derived from the manipulation of sail surfaces, from studying the vectors of wind, boat, and sail so keenly, have imprinted unconscious patterns upon Pratt's imagination. He is too sensitive to weights, divisions, balances, pressures, strains, and compressions, not to have been affected, especially since many of his aesthetic forms derive from machinery and engineered forms.

More important, perhaps, has been the deepening of his understanding of the relationship between land and sea. From a point farther out to sea, which his increased confidence in sailing permits, he now has a clearer perspective of behemoth and leviathan, Job's two great imponderables of existence. They were always there, of course, but in the Newfoundland of his boyhood Pratt was more engrossed by the often miniature scale of the wildlife and flora of the land, the endless variety of brooks, hills, ponds, tundra, cities, farms, and forests. By contrast, the boundless, insistent sea, infinitely variable in its monotony of sound and movement, has enthralled his adult mind. In recent years, he has reassessed the proportions and the scale of land seen across water, examined the surfaces of each and the contentions between them. In his mind, as in his pictures, the view over water is a journey through time and, therefore, a timeless link connecting past and future in the present. He takes the measure of sea and land with clock as well as ruler. The sea encompasses many great mysteries, and these mysteries surface in Pratt the painter and image-maker.

*　　*　　*

Delacroix once noted, in a moment of candour, that every artist was first an amateur. Pratt is no exception, although he has the excuse of having started while still a boy and the distinction of having surveyed the boundaries of his style before he went to art school. His first impulse was to use painting as a record, to trap places in the memory, to 'make things look square and solid,' as he has in works such as *Battery Road* (page 39) and *Winter, St. John's Harbour*. Recording certain subjects requires respect for them. It also manifests a desire to control and to shape the future through selection, emphasis, and the imposition of values. Even the paintings of Pratt's teenage years display more than 'fact'; they have a spirit of invention, reaction, and licence. A picture called *Death of the Mate* depicts one of a pair of geese being shot out of the sky. It foreshadows Pratt's adult preoccupation with loss, a melancholy attitude to youth, and a fear of age.

With self-instruction and the well-intentioned artistic examples of his family, Pratt propelled himself along with adolescent enthusiasm until he enrolled in engineering at Memorial University in 1953 with a view to entering the family business in steel and hardware. There, over the drafting table, he became fascinated more by drawing than by engineering. To judge from the drawings done since, it was a particular and idiosyncratic kind of drawing, not at all what he would have encountered in art school. He was mesmerized by geometric forms, triangles, circles, and cones, and by the puzzles, ambiguities, and illusions these could create. The relationship between scale and size was explored; surface was pitted against volume, two-dimensional pattern against three-dimensional representation, appearance against reality. The most crucial thing was that Pratt drew all these mathematical structures with the most delicate and sensuous of surfaces. To this day, he continues to find delight and enjoyment in the actual, physical act of painting or drawing.

The stab at engineering was short-lived, and Pratt's subsequent student days in science, medicine, and literature at Mount Allison University in New Brunswick were erratic and confused. In 1957, when he finally decided on a profession, got married, and settled on the Glasgow School of Art to try to become an artist, he really was one already. His aims and methods were generally formed, and he already knew where and how he wanted to work. All four years of his formal art school training, two in

Glasgow and two back at Mount Allison, served to reinforce what he had already determined for himself. True, he knew practically nothing of art history, he was technically limited, and he had little experience to build on. Nevertheless, his associates in Glasgow thought his work very 'American,' which is not only an indication of an established and authentic kind of expression, but also proof that the only influence on him to that point had been the early American watercolour tradition. The ideas of the Impressionists, Cubists, Abstract Expressionists, or even of the Group of Seven, were a closed book.

Works done in 1957 through 1961 confirmed Pratt's mature style and refined it while he was still formally a student but, for the most part, painting, drawing, and making silkscreen prints alone at home. *Haystacks in December* and *Boat in Sand* (pages 43, 47), sold to fellow students at twenty-five dollars a print, are examples of his early originality and generosity.

The fact that little work exists for 1962 and 1963, when Pratt was employed by Memorial University as a curator and teacher, is an indication that his reflective way of working requires time and peace. When he finally found his feet in 1964, after moving to his home on the Salmonier the year before, the full range of his concerns was instantly evident. At that point, his change in intent and purpose made him an artist rather than an illustrator; his urge to record was sublimated as he moved from the documentary form into the form of the elegy.

Canadian traditions barely touched Pratt until the 1960s. His formation as an artist is an odd but strong mixture of amateurism, which made and makes him a self-reliant thinker; of American romantic regional realism of the nineteenth and early twentieth centuries, especially as manifested in Edward Hopper, whose attitudes match Pratt's cast of mind; of European academism, in which he was steeped in Glasgow; and of Italian primitivism, as in the works of Giotto and Masaccio who enjoyed a revival of popularity in the forties and fifties.

Pratt was legislated into Canadian citizenship at the impressionable age of thirteen when Newfoundland joined Canada in 1949 and he became a Canadian artist by the sole virtue of his change in nationality. Attempts to lump him in with other Maritime artists have a certain political rationale but little artistic purpose because, among his Canadian contemporaries, he is most drawn to abstract painters like Charles Gagnon and Yves Gaucher or to such experimental spirits as Iain Baxter and Michael Snow.

Even a cursory study of Pratt's work reveals a steadfast purpose, a grain along which his ideas run. An emphasis on design governs both the mental sifting and sorting of his attitude toward a subject, idea, or feeling and the subsequent physical labour by which he renders his concept visually. In the first instance, an image may develop from either a direct experience or a concatenation of experiences, memories, and thoughts, sometimes prompted by photographs. In the second instance, with half of his work already done in his head, Pratt proceeds to draw, plan, and measure. His drawings, at first coarse and small, are later refined as he proceeds toward the larger work. At this stage the imperatives of art and its traditions come into play, and Pratt employs various techniques and methods that may simplify or alter the painting, print, or drawing quite considerably but that still drive steadily toward his initial impulse and purpose. Even when he draws for its own sake, especially his figure drawings, or applies himself to making silkscreen prints or collages, Pratt's visual language is always recognizable. How he deploys his visual ideas through omission, repetition, and colour is an important key to his work. A persistent tendency to work in series also unlocks a truth about his ruminative progress.

Of greater importance, however, are the intangible factors in Pratt's works. To resolve some of the contradictions that art and life confront him with, Pratt adopts an ironic tone, which permits more than one interpretation. Irony, in titles which are ambiguous or images which can stand as natural facts or as symbols, is a quality common to most of his works. At the same time, the representational clarity of Pratt's images is not in doubt. He depicts known objects, often to emphasize the way he sees them, that is, as metaphors of perception. Pratt's vision sometimes has the clarity that a telescope gives, but as often, he portrays drifting snow, fog, or darkness, elements which impede or obscure sight. All these qualities, taken collectively, culminate in Pratt's elegiac mode of expression, a form that meets his need to express his profound sense of death and of the outer dimensions of life. Pratt's works are thus a reflection of his mind and thought more than a representation of reality: they are metaphors of his experiences and insights, time-markers or epitaphs for his ideas, which reside beneath representation.

Of the many mysteries imbedded in any work of art, what people want most to know is the hidden, furthest point of origin. What place or experience, what vision or belief, triggered the artist's imagination? With Pratt's regional emphasis and factual images, it must seem that by comparing a photograph of this house or that stretch of water with a painting, one could judge how truthfully he had dealt with it. Barring a few early exceptions, however, Pratt's images have no specific locations, despite what the titles may suggest. Each image has many ancestors. By the time an initial thought has been meditated on, expanded, turned around in the mind, and chipped and chiselled by collision with new thoughts and experiences, it has taken on a life of its own, quite separate from its starting point. Nearly all of Pratt's works are fantasies or fabrications, constructions of the mind based on, or abstracted from, personal events or ideas.

A curious and revealing example of Pratt's attitudes and methods lies behind the print *Hawke Bay* (page 165). In 1972 I joined Pratt, his father, brother, and uncle on their trip 'down the Labrador' aboard his uncle's motor launch *Hemmer Jane*. It was July and, although the worst of the ice was past for the year, icebergs still dotted the horizon and peppered the radar screen. We were often close enough to be dwarfed by their vastness and intrigued by their subtle spectrum of colours, from a diamond-blue white through aquamarine green to a frothy brown.

One of our early stops was at the ancient Labrador village of Battle Harbour, where we were sucked back in time as we explored its decayed and scattered cemetery and visited its weathered but clean and simple parish church, which Pratt photographed extensively. We bought old postcards from the post office at the general store. Seal corpses by the dock, freshly skinned, echoed an older way of life.

A day or so later, *Hemmer Jane* was bunting her way,

21

Christopher Pratt, *St. Mary's Bay*, 1977

JOHN REEVES

Age 5, On Le Marchant Road, St. John's, 1940

*I never paint specifics. I shouldn't say 'never.'
Sometimes I come close, and when I do,
I think it's the weakest part of my work.
But everything I do is informed and influenced
by a range of experiences, encounters, and
acquaintances. It's a collective, a generality.
So there's ambiguity. I sometimes make an
effort not to represent a particular time of day
or a particular season. Because if a painting
has no time, it has all time. Nearly everything I do is a mental or spiritual collage.
Not in the sense that I take a wall from here
and a window from there, but a collage conjured up from reactions and experiences that
go back a long way, sometimes to childhood.*

Making silkscreen prints for the limited edition of *Christopher Pratt*, St. Mary's Bay, 1979

On the *Hemmer Jane* with his father, J. K. Pratt, 1966

Age 10, With Salmon, at Placentia, 1945

With Mary, Salmonier River, St. Mary's Bay, 1981

with pugnacious grace, through the cold, clear water of Hawke Bay. We were on our way to visit a defunct whaling factory. It was a bright, clear, sunny day, and the water was full of the pulsating, luminous umbrellas of jellyfish. We passed through the narrow gut entrance to Hawke Harbour, circled about by high rocky hills, and we marvelled that larger ships, whale carcasses lashed to their sides, could have navigated into this old whale-rendering station. Not that many years earlier, the whole station had itself been stripped to a skeleton by fire, leaving a spectacular, incongruous tangle of sagging pipes, leaning flues, rusting tanks, flanges, ramps, and fittings, now brilliantly set against the grass and nodding flowers.

Off to the side was the fire's only survivor, the dull railway-red clapboard bunkhouse, trimmed in white. Inside its dingy confines was the epicentre of whatever experience we took away from Hawke Harbour. There, jammed fifteen to a small room, the whalers' wooden bunks mouldered, three deep, like shelves or galleys, with one small window and one small stove to share. Crudely scratched into the walls of this warren were the poignant diary entries of a miserable way of life: days left to serve, no mail from home, Willie a truant to his rabbit snares, and other resonating but unprintable views about Hawke Harbour and its grindingly inhuman treatment of men.

Pratt was stunned and silent. He stood transfixed, etching it all on the back of his mind. The whole experience, perhaps the more forceful for being unexpected, was like exploring a major archeological site of a way of life that was both gone and yet within memory. It seemed as if, sequestered away up here, Hawke Harbour

had been forgotten on purpose.

After our trip, Pratt did several pencil sketches. One was a whistle-clean diagram of the triple-stacked bunks. A few months had gone by, but he was excited about its potential as a painting or a print. Instead, other images emerged. The idea, whatever it was, simply was not ready to crystallize.

Though Hawke Harbour was often talked about over the years, the possibility of it becoming more than a tentative drawing became increasingly remote. The indelible experience remained, the basis of a complex idea, but the bunks, separated from their squalor and their literary descant, were either not suggestive enough, or perhaps too oppressive to dwell upon. For Pratt's generalized artistic statements, this subject was too specific, too close to propaganda.

When Pratt handed me the print *Hawke Bay*, nearly eight years after our visit, I found the subject surprising. I remembered that the series of prints, *Ice*, *Strait of Belle Isle*, and *Labrador Current* (pages 83, 85, 87), inspired by this and other trips, was originally to have had a fourth member, which simply had not materialized. The artistic or formal ancestor might be traced to these in part. But the subject! Between an expanse of calm water and a serene sky squats an implacable and impenetrable bank of fog, over which is a glimpse of icy cliffs. Although we joked about the title and the cavalier change to winter from a full summer day, Pratt remarked, with some emphasis, that when he conceived the print he had had a strong, pervading sense of the feeling engendered by Hawke Harbour. Something in the shapes and tensions of the picture came from that experience, and the image, at least in part, is a metaphor of it, a sharing, perhaps, of the cold splendour of that wild shore with the men who had lived and endured there.

*   *   *

When Pratt makes a painting, or an 'object' as he constantly calls his works, he believes design to be the central element. The core and foundation of his art is design, and it is a moot point whether Pratt creates a design for a subject or whether a subject is chosen for a design. A work of art, for Pratt, has to stand on its own merits which are independent of its source. It is both astonishing and significant how often pure design factors are the final determinants in Pratt's work.

In many works of art, the design is a composition of organic forms, weighed by the eye and dependent upon how pigment is handled. In Pratt's case, a geometric structure is engineered, stressed, proportioned, calculated, and balanced with the care one would bring to the design of a bridge or the cutting of a diamond. Precision in this degree means measurement, and Pratt charts his course in mathematical detail, computing sections, recessions, intersections, and focal points with actuarial glee, although he invariably exercises a final visual correction. He uses squares, circles, $\sqrt{5}$ rectangles, fulcrums, levers, incidences of reflection, and golden section divisions, because they have served other artists successfully in the past and serve him well in organizing shapes mentally and graphically. He points to the composition points of an equilateral triangle as if simply doing so were ample justification of aesthetic rightness, a self-evident truth.

In his earlier work, Pratt tended to accept the dictates of what he saw, such as the random states of the windows in *Grosvenor Crescent* (page 41) of 1957. Since then, however, Pratt has done all the dictating to make subjects conform to his priorities in design and his insistence on simplicity. His work throughout the sixties shows this, although the angles and recessions of the late sixties, for example those in *Barn and Cellar* (page 81), have since given way to the directness of absolute frontality. This frontality tends to flatten the picture and bring the image flush with the picture plane, or at least close enough to permit only a shallow ledge of recession space, as in *March Night*, *Shop on an Island*, *Front Room*, and *Window on the Stairs* (pages 135, 89, 115, 91). And thus we return to the surface again, where illusion wrestles perpetually with two-dimensional design. Pratt revealed how his work was put together when he disassembled *The House at Path End* (page 141) into its self-contained, abstract, two-dimensional components, the most striking of which is *The House at Path End: Clapboard* (page 140). An emphasis on design tends to be sharply anti-realistic, a quality that achieves the generality Pratt seeks and perhaps a flavour of mystery.

Design factors have also led Pratt to diptychs and triptychs, works subdivided into two or three panels, which may look in several directions at once but are maintained as a unity. The model for this convention is the screen in eastern art or the altarpiece in western art. Pratt used the device in *Bay* (page 109) and in *Parish Hall* (page 117) to reinforce and extend the images, to provide a container that lends complexity to what appears to be too simple a subject. In *Federal Area* (page 121), the different panels act as a counterpoint to each other and provide contrasts in scale, size, colour, and mood. The two-dimensional surface is emphasized by multiple panels, a characteristic of the early Italian primitives, whose works exerted an important influence on Pratt's artistic development. Their precision, structural compositions, and architectural settings appealed to him, and so did their stylized treatment of objects and their limited depth of field.

Painters have used photography in various ways since it was invented and so does Pratt. His interest in visual records gives him a natural entry to the medium, and he uses snapshots as reminders. Sometimes he explores or examines a subject by photographing it; sometimes he confirms or verifies what he has already designed. Like a photographer, Pratt fiddles with square-angled mats to isolate compositions within a picture. He photographs his models for reference and study, but not to draw or paint from since he finds the emotional presence of a woman necessary to the vitality of his drawing.

Often he will photograph a subject over many weeks or months before he makes a picture. I think here of *The Sheep*, *Clothesline*, and *Parish Hall* (pages 93, 59, 117), each of which has a host of models, observed and photographed all over Newfoundland. Chiefly, however, Pratt uses photographs or slides as a filing cabinet of images, which he riffles through at leisure. Doing so produces a clash of disparate thoughts, odd juxtapositions of images, and a sharpened memory, any of which might suggest a new insight, problem, or opportunity. But Pratt also has a keen interest and some involvement in photography as an independent art, and he views photographs as we view his paintings, as bridges over time that allow the past to be present, old but unweathered, ageless.

If the mental preparation for a painting is extended over a sometimes lengthy period, so too does the physical execution proceed through various rigorous steps. The beginning, most often, is with tiny, rough sketches in ink or pencil, in which only the essential features of a subject are seen. Pratt describes these little chits as a sort of shorthand, reminders of things that they do not necessarily describe. But no matter how developed an image may be in the mind, this initial visualization on paper prompts a host of new considerations, a shift of weight, the elimination—practically never any addition—of certain features, a reorganization of the elements, or a change in the point of view. In the sequence of studies for *Demolitions on the South Side* (page 45), for example, Pratt has hauled the whole subject around from a three-quarter profile to a frontal view and eliminated many elements that were important in the first sketch, such as the street lights and the road over the hill.

Pratt next moves to a more precise drawing, a clean, clear prototype. Here, measurement and accuracy begin to be considered, and the various components begin to fit into a tight visual format. Even at this point, as in the studies for *Institution* (page 107), Pratt juggles the pieces around freely, no longer worried about their conformity to things he may have seen at different times and places but intensely concerned with their relationship to what he is now trying to fit together on a piece of paper. At this stage, when he has struck a workable solution, he may do a detailed study on squared paper, such as those for *Coast Winter* and *Labrador Sea* (page 164), to assist with the translation to a larger canvas or silk stencil, a technique that would seem old-fashioned in lesser hands.

The full-scale version may force further, quite often

drastic, changes in design, though not in concept. One example is the interim state of *House in August* (page 76). The asymmetry of the initial design, generally acceptable to Pratt, did not catch the still point of summer that he wanted, and he proceeded to develop a perfectly balanced, symmetrical, and flatter solution, one more consistent with his general goals and intentions. In *Station* (page 99), to take another example, Pratt had originally planned to have a railway engine with the familiar Canadian National logo visible through the window, but once he painted it in he felt uncomfortable with it. Logo and engine were scrubbed out and replaced by the night, which reflected the lonely room to itself and seized the anonymity of stations with more force than the engine could have conveyed.

Pratt's compulsion to simplify has led him to other major revisions. *Night Window* (page 11) was originally conceived and painted with the artist and then a model reflected in the window. When he removed the figures, Pratt also peeled away an unnecessary layer of ambiguity. Viewers would no longer see the artist watching the artist watching himself, but rather, would enter into a conspiracy of perception with the artist and would themselves become the seeing but unseen eye of the painting, looking into themselves. *Subdivision* (page 114) originally had a female figure staring at the viewer/artist, but the effect seemed such an indecent and reciprocal invasion of privacy that Pratt painted her out.

A more dramatic example of recasting an initial concept lies behind *Young Girl with Seashells*. This work was first conceived as a panel in a projected suite on the four seasons. It depicted a young man and woman gathering apples, using the girl's skirt as a basket. The orchard setting proved too amorphous and was replaced by the doorway of a house. Then the girl was moved inside the doorway and her partner obliterated, with the orchard in the background being displaced by the seashore. By that time neither red nor yellow nor green apples served either design or symbolic purposes. Something white was called for, but the overt symbolism of eggs was rejected, finally, in favour of clam shells.

In more recent works than those just cited, the process of shuffling and rearranging continues. *Me and Bride* (page 6) of 1981 ran a gamut of alterations over a period of three years or so. Originally it began as a four-panel night painting of the artist and a model (Bride is the model's name) reflected in the four-sectioned window of Pratt's studio. First, a fifth panel was added because the design seemed to require it. Then a verandah was added behind the reflected artist and model. That overlay was unsatisfactory and while the verandah was retained, in a redesigned form, the idea of a reflection was dispensed with, leaving the artist and model as positive not mirrored subjects, now outside in the night. The only vestige of the first impulse is that the artist is still shown as left-handed whereas Pratt is right-handed.

Although Pratt sketches while planning a visual idea for a painting, the drawings he makes for their own sake are also an important part of his work. A few, such as *Gregory's Punt* and *Shed Door* (pages 78, 80), are slightly polychromed and really paintings as much as drawings, but the majority are either in pencil or pencil on prepared paper. They range from architectural subjects to still lifes and landscapes, although most of them are of the female figure. Their structural basis is strict and imposing. These drawings are, with few exceptions, completed works, conceived for the space they occupy, often preceded by studies, and as scrupulously executed as Pratt's larger paintings or silkscreen prints.

The figure drawings, despite the sensuous poses and surfaces, often convey a stilted quality, an impression that the figures were assembled in sections. There are two reasons for this, applicable to both the figure drawings and the figure paintings. First, Pratt flattens and generalizes his images, and when this tendency is transferred to human figures, it tends to rob them of their individuality. This stylized treatment, most evident in the prosthetic elbows and knees, is directly opposed to the sense of roundness and fullness that figures and faces demand. The conflict can be seen in *Summer Place* (page 144), where the girl's arm does not recede to the shoulder and neck, and the perspective of the basin and stand is too steeply raked. Second, Pratt does not draw with the immediate, calligraphic fluency of a Picasso or a Rembrandt. His painstaking and calculating method creates figures that sometimes resemble mannikins with soft skins stretched over wooden armatures, and these may occasionally live up to his betraying description of them as maps of the human figure.

Pratt's usual thoroughness, as it informs his figure work, leads him into complicated equations of balance in regard to lines, shapes, and shading. These subtle considerations naturally attenuate his statements and reduce the possibility or the appearance of spontaneity. However, the intensity of his approach and the depth of his insight is not diminished because of his elaborate care. What he is driving at is as much a psychological statement of the person, as is the case in *Me and Bride* (page 6), as it is a treatment of physical characteristics. Besides, there are enough exceptions, such as *Woman in Black* (page 131) to indicate that particular poses and models trigger quite different responses. Pratt would prefer, so he has said, to adopt more often a shorter, more lyric form of expression, but he finds it difficult to submerge intellectual and formal responses and allow his emotional responses full rein. Yet over the years his commitment to figure drawings and paintings has won him increasing freedom and ease in execution. His latest drawings are more inventive, assured, and uninhibited than anything done before 1980.

*　　　*　　　*

The most widely known of Pratt's works are his silkscreen prints. Despite their visual similarity to his paintings, Pratt uses the medium in a highly individual way. The usual method is simple and widely used in commerce. Generally, artists have stencils made by technicians or by photographic means from a painting or watercolour. Most silkscreen prints are, therefore, only reproductions made under varying degrees of supervision and control. Pratt, however, paints each stencil, up to as many as fifteen per image, directly on the silk and labours through every stage of the printing process himself. Each print, consequently, is the product of his hand just as is a painting or a watercolour.

Between 1968 and 1974, Pratt completed six silkscreen prints based on nineteenth-century Newfoundland stamps. This sudden affection for codfish and Queen Victoria struck some Pratt admirers as an aberration, and a sentimental one at that, though it appeased, perhaps, his anti-Confederate relatives. Pratt's interest in philately led him to these works and, subsequently, to a few years' service on Canada's postage stamp design committee. In his eyes the stamps were beautiful objects, well designed, and part of a proud pre-Confederation heritage which he wished to salute. Typically, he produced them according to precise philatelic models, bearing aspects of stamp manufacture in mind, testing various colours of issue, and classifying his work according to philatelic tradition. The *1887 10¢ Black* (page 172), for example, was executed as a block of nine, *The Stamp* (page 173), in a block of four, and there are three colour variants for both *Victoria Regina* and *Prince Albert* (page 171).

The stamp prints offered Pratt a radical change in method, since all except *The Stamp* are only one stencil, and the calligraphy, as he happily confessed, is not even his own. He once described them as Newfoundland pop art, but they are, their scale alone being the difference, one of Pratt's solitary skirmishes with overt realism. With their size giving them iconic stature, they will be seen, in time, not as a tangent to but as a significant part of his work. Pratt's affinity for design, tradition, and heraldry made him the natural choice to create the new provincial flag for Newfoundland or Labrador. Adopted in 1980, it is one that will wear well through the years.

If anything that Pratt makes qualifies as an 'object,' to use his term, it is his collages, to date very few in number. In 1972 and 1973, he created some that relate to the prints *Ice*, *Strait of Belle Isle*, and *Labrador Current* (pages 83, 85, 87) and to the painting *Bay* (page 109). Several more, a year later, were exploratory prototypes for *Ocean Racer* (page 119). Pratt makes them from plain strips of differently coloured, carefully cut illustration board, arranged for proportion, balance, and weight of both area and colour. The collages are Pratt playing his Euclidean games with the shapes and colours of his other work, reaching in them a totally flat, abstract surface. These works achieve two things: the aesthetic goal of absolute frontality and the illusion of recession. The purity and simplicity that Pratt seeks in his work are manifest here.

As most artists move from medium to medium, their expression varies, pushed along by the demands and suggestions of the material itself. What an artist will venture in oil, he may not try in watercolour and vice versa. Pratt says that he selects his medium for each idea with care, that he welcomes the opportunity to change, and that he feels quite differently about each medium. Yet setting aside the drawings, what is striking about Pratt's oil paintings, watercolours, and silkscreen prints, is how homogeneous they are despite the medium and despite the artist's feeling of difference. The most obvious reason for this curious similarity is that neither Pratt's hand nor his intention changes fundamentally as he shifts from one medium to another. Whichever he chooses is pressed into the mould of his purpose, and thus, the effect remains essentially constant.

Whether Pratt is working at a drawing, a print, a collage, or a painting, his artistic vocabulary is nearly always the same. His most obvious rhetorical device is the elision of detail, a practice that stands opposed to the impression his work gives of being objective, precise, and inclusive. In his earlier watercolour *Window with Lace Curtain* of 1964, for example, Pratt has given all the proof needed that he is technically capable of depicting peeling paint, broken glass, and cobwebs, the staples of what he calls the 'barn and buggy school of painting.' The logical assumption about this particular work, a false one as it turns out, is that the artist has copied a model with more or less success. One reason that Pratt quickly abandoned this low level of imitation was that it was misleading for his more difficult purpose. Pratt wants an image somewhere between a specific example and a totally abstract precept. He therefore describes paradigms of a subject, purified examples that are not subject to the small, distracting imperfections that one member of a species might display. Although the intimate, wall-papered interiors and the delicate apparel in his nude paintings add distinct tenderness to *Young Woman Dressing* and *Young Woman with a Slip* (pages 63, 65), their Galatean stiffness is largely due to this compulsion to abstract and to generalize.

Pratt omits details for a number of reasons related to design, the foremost of which is simplification. The practice is an extension of the conceptual and composi-tional simplification noted earlier. In the painting *Window with a Blind* (page 90), the cords and the window latch were eliminated, for both would have detracted from the rhythm of horizontal and vertical elements, and neither is part of an essential definition of either window or blind. Similarly, in *Railway* (page 155), bed plates or spikes were unnecessary to trigger recognition and would distract from the horizontal line of the rail so important to the design. For the same reason, there are no footprints in *The Lynx* (page 51) and no shadows under the sheets in *Clothesline* (page 59). Such examples can be found in many works. In every case, the process of reduction and subtraction contributes to the sense of mystery in Pratt's work, for the very omission, even when not immediately noticed, stirs curiosity. It is a device that is both forceful and provocative: by revealing aspects of the subject through elision, Pratt actually enhances appreciation of it.

Pratt frequently chooses subjects in which there are repeated shapes. The most obvious of these are the myriad waves of the sea, but one notes, too, the spokes in a bannister or railing, window panes, wainscotting, floor boards, wallpaper patterns, Venetian blind slats, sections of a radiator, shelves, stairs, railway ties, and acres of clapboard. These repeated forms, a kind of visual drum-ming, are seldom exactly identical. If they are seen from fairly close, the perspective alters. But occasionally, as in the magnificent *Breakwater* (page 139), all sixty-five pilings are perpendicular to the eye. Like a refrain in music, these visual repetitions become a hypnotic chant-ing, intended to elevate our perceptions from one plane to another.

Colour in Pratt's work is so unobtrusive that it is either the last detail noticed or one comes away without any sense of colour at all. This reflects the role Pratt has assigned to colour rather than his actual use of it. Like the accompaniment to a song, colour is subordinate to design. Chiefly, it is there to establish the mood or tone of a work.

The whitened hues are manipulated and graded to enhance forms and their relationships.

What is strangest about Pratt's distinctive colour, however, is that he does not use local colour, the actual hue of an object, any more than he uses a specific place or object. Rather, he selects from a narrow range of blues, greys, greens, and browns, for the most part, and applies them to forms that he has already bleached of colour. The values of his colours are also close and reined in, and they are never keyed very highly.

Nevertheless, Pratt's colours can be as emphatic as they are subdued. The large expanses of brown in *The Visitor* and *Basement Flat* (pages 143, 154) are examples, although the powerful blue-black in *The House at Path End*, *Station*, and *March Night* (pages 141, 99, 135) would serve the point as well. The pinks in *The Bed* (page 95) generate an antiseptic austerity that even Pratt's architectural works do not have. But the primrose pink suffusion in *Wall Facing West* (page 161) is a new note in Pratt's work, one with tantalizing potential. That Pratt thinks of colour for its symbolic and metaphoric value is indicated, too, in the odd green and black combination in *Landing* (page 113). Colour supports and reinforces Pratt's artistic intent, as one can observe most clearly in *March Crossing* (page 151), with its level, unperturbed composition, its gently shaded tones that give a touch and smell of sea air, of light and reflection, however artificial.

Finally, in three recent paintings, Pratt has turned again to the practice of working in series. This is not uncommon among artists at any time, but in Pratt the full realization of a series is rare, even while the suggestion of close linkage is frequent. For example, the projected 'seasons' suite of four in 1964 produced one painting and one never-released print, and the projected suite of four prints in 1972 ended up as three: *Ice*, *Strait of Belle Isle*, and *Labrador Current* (pages 83, 85, 87). Only the matched trio of prints created for the limited edition of *Christopher Pratt* in 1980—*Western Shore*, *Labrador Sea*, and *Hawke Bay* (pages 166, 167, 168)—and the three paintings *Trunk*, *Bed and Blind*, and *Dresser and Dark Window* (pages 167, 168, 169), all of 1981, were completed as initially planned. The truth about unrealized or incipient series, where intention faltered in execution, can be gleaned from an examination of Pratt's works and from his own confessions on the subject.

Relationships among paintings completed at different times are complex, but there is a kinship in idea, composition, and treatment behind, say, *The Lynx* and *The Sheep* (pages 51, 93), even though they were done nearly six years apart. The stamps, also done over six years, are an obvious example of his persistent delving into one particular aesthetic idea and with each new expression of it, enlarging his understanding of it. More subtle, perhaps, are the mental connections among certain of the architectural subjects such as *House and Barn*, *Barn and Cellar*, *Clothesline*, and *Two Houses in the Spring* (pages 48, 81, 59, 73), or such as *Wall Facing West* and *March Night* (pages 161, 135), to cite an example which may still be extended from studies already finished. Various studies for *Ocean Racer* (page 119) might easily have become full-scale works in their own right. And in Pratt's ruminative way, further consideration is far from impossible.

Trunk, *Bed and Blind*, and *Dresser and Dark Window* were conceived, started, and painted together. They form

31

a suite of similar subjects, recollections of furniture in a room, and they are all the same size and tone. They are reminiscent in some ways of such works as *Cupboard* or *The Bed* (pages 129, 95) but, like *Western Shore*, *Labrador Sea*, and *Hawke Bay*, they are more accessible and less severe or anxious than works done a few years earlier. Together, *Trunk*, *Bed and Blind*, and *Dresser and Dark Window* make a larger statement, a more extended proposition, than would be possible if each was considered individually. They have a sum larger than their parts, just as Pratt's works have more resonance collectively than separately because his vision is one of connections, of relationships, and of wholeness.

The figure drawings of 1981 and 1982 are also part of Pratt's tendency to work in series, more so than his drawings during the sixties and seventies which tended to be solo performances or preparations for other works. Along with the above three paintings and *Me and Bride* (page 6), these drawings stand apart somewhat from earlier work and suggest a new strength and depth in Pratt's understanding of himself and of his art.

The range of expression and the directness of approach are evidence of a freedom which surpasses previous work by an appreciable degree. Pratt's various techniques of elision, repetition, simplification, and his choices of colour are still at work, but his vision has recently taken on a clarity and a force which surpass his earlier conceptions by a good measure.

The whole complex process, from concept to finished work or works, even when it advances smoothly, is enormously time-consuming as Pratt inches his circumspect way along, studying each detail to the last notch, revising, hesitating, and justifying. His record for an oil painting, he once told me, was a flat-out three weeks; normally work is protracted over several months, and this accounts for Pratt's relatively low production of three or four large paintings a year. But these are minor considerations beside the dominance of Pratt's continued variety of designs and subjects and the strength of his unflickering vision.

The intuitive devices in Pratt's art, as opposed to the manual techniques, are more difficult to recognize and to analyze. Pratt compounds the difficulty, though not consciously, by throwing up an ironic screen in front of his work. Irony is saying one thing while meaning something else. The use of irony is a constant in Pratt's speech and in his art and lends itself directly to the device of metaphor. By presenting his images as natural facts on one level, Pratt disguises moral and social comment. On another level, we sense that his facts have been filtered through the bloodstream of his experience, and we accept them as facts of his imagination. In this way they can be presented in an altered form, cleansed and unified by his mind's eye. Pratt's ironic tone comes by playing one mode of presentation against the other.

T*he Lynx* is, on one level, a nature painting. It is stylized in colour and detail, as are Pratt's other works, but is a factual statement all the same. The long, flat plain, the distant horizon, and the scale of the tiny shrubs make the animal look large and menacing. In fact, the lynx is a small feline, and these particular Newfoundland bushes are fully grown at about a foot in height.

On another level, *The Lynx* is a self-portrait. Detached, despite its tension, the picture represents, perhaps, some aspect of the artist's own character. Or it may represent a side of nature that lurks in many of Pratt's paintings, a violent and destructive side. Finally, there is the level of the traditional literary and artistic antecedents, which one cannot ignore.

*T*he *Sheep* is another example of such a work, firmly rooted in Pratt's locale with its pole fences. Though not overtly symbolic, it too invites speculation about its meaning. The viewer can be charged with reading too much symbolic meaning into these pictures, or, conversely, with ignoring their symbolic import by taking them solely at face value.

Titles have the same concrete quality as do Pratt's images and are often cast in the same ironic mould. Obviously, as the example of *Hawke Bay* shows, they can be chosen with a degree of poetic licence. Like some designs awaiting subjects, Pratt has titles awaiting subjects. A title may be either the starting point or the conclusion of a work. *The Sheep*, *The Lynx*, and *Plough in a Storm* (page 71) are descriptive and seem specific but are not. Others like *Apartment*, *Landing*, and *Institution* (pages 125, 113, 107) are emphatically generalized and neutral. One like *Subdivision* (page 114) is ambiguous. And some titles appear to be giving exact identification when they are, in fact, drawing down a veil of anonymity. *Shop on Sunday* (page 69), for example, was titled after the work was finished. For design purposes, Pratt drew closed blinds on the windows, not only to stress the frontality and the shallowness of the space, but also to avoid having to contend with the stuff usually found in store windows. But he was apprehensive that the work would be interpreted as a social commentary on an abandoned outport shop. Perhaps he had been criticized about an earlier work, *Outport Business* (page 55), in which the windows are both open and empty. With a deft title, Pratt provided an aesthetic as well as a sociological solution.

Coley's Point and *The House at Path End* (pages 103, 141) are fantasies given known place names. Geographically, there is actually no *Labrador Sea* (page 164), and *Labrador Current* (page 87) is an invisible motion, an abstraction that, like the wind, cannot be portrayed. *Cape St. Mary's* (page 132) appropriates a lighthouse form found throughout Newfoundland. Yet these titles suit the pictures and are integral to the compositions. If one ignores the titles, aspects of the works that are important may be missed. But if they are taken too seriously, the viewer will find himself being quietly mocked.

Pratt's use of metaphor, the way the mind has of creating an equivalence from experience to expression through images, words, or sounds, is central to his significance as an artist. The clues to this turn of mind are so liberally strewn about that, once noticed, no other way of considering his work seems possible.

*L*ike other artists whose paramount concern is with perception, Pratt is preoccupied with the paraphernalia of his vision: cyclopean lighthouses, arbitrary light, flawless reflections, doors, windows, shutters, screens, and blinds. These are the eyes of the domestic environment, the metaphors of perception. In the same vein, though in a demonic mode, are the metaphors of the dark, uncontrollable side of nature: fog, drifting snow, winter, and darkness, interchangeable elements which figure in a surprising number of Pratt's works. The similarity of the snow blustering around the truck in *Plough in a Storm* (page 71) and the fog swirling across the sea in *Western Shore* (page 163) is striking.

Frequently, we seem to be viewing subjects under a microscope or magnifying glass, where scale seems slightly larger than life, as in *The Lynx*. Sometimes we seem to be viewing through a telescope, which, theoretically, is looking back in time as do those through which astronomers scan the heavens. Pratt's images of the past are presented in this fashion, still fresh and crisp, without the distortions of memory or the patina of age. In this way, the spirit of the past, rather than the past itself, can be called up.

In many works, such as *Good Friday*, *Sunday Afternoon*, *March Night*, and *Wall Facing West* (pages 111, 102, 135, 161), there is a sharp dividing line both in the thought and the composition, a device that is a metaphor for time and often represented by a contrast between near and far, which in Pratt's mind is also a contrast between the immediate and the eternal. The line is a metaphysical edge or brink that divides existence into two distinct states or zones, like a riptide in time. This sense of edge is paramount in Pratt's art. Pratt has told me that he finds new snow nearly impossible to draw and that he can wring little meaning out of it until it has melted a little and formed an edge. Drawing needs an edge, clarity needs an edge, and Pratt's brand of expression needs an edge to define itself.

Could it be that there is a direct equation between space, time, light, and mood? Is limited space a way to describe the shortness of time? Is darkness pessimistic? Is bright light stretched or extended time and an optimistic mood? The correlations are not wholly fortuitous—the works are too deliberate for that—and would not be inconsistent with Pratt's work up to this point.

Pratt's metaphoric intent is evident in his choice of subjects. He usually chooses nature at its most typical—a calm sea, the deepest point of a dark night, a bright noon with the sun at its height, the turning point of morning or evening as night ends or begins. *Light Northeast*, *House and Barn*, and *Three O'Clock* (pages 159, 48, 67) all illustrate this tendency. Except for a few adolescent works and *Plough in a Storm*, nature's abnormalities and extremes of violence are avoided. Pratt also avoids satire and sarcasm. There are no light or humorous touches, no amusing or witty references to other art, except for the wry affection in the stamp prints or perhaps a tongue-in-cheek title. Nevertheless, the brooding potential for shattering change is often implied. Subjects are caught at the apogee of their course, when change seems to be both imminent and inevitable.

Pratt's search for a moment out of time, the meditative and introspective quality of his work, his use of irony and metaphor, have all led him to an elegiac form of expression. An elegy is, in the narrow sense, a lament for the death of a person, and the form is used by poets to meditate on the loss or passing of a spirit or an order. Coleridge defined the elegy as 'the form of poetry natural to the reflective mind' and thought that the poet could treat any subject in that mode so long as it made reference to the poet himself. As used by Pratt, in his pastoral setting, it is a jeremiad for the spirit of life abandoning nature. Symbolically, this departure is represented by night or winter. When nature is gripped in stasis, so that it can be turned around and contemplated at will, so too is time, by extrapolation, suspended.

In Pratt the man and Pratt the artist the sense of loss is deep and abiding. The faded tradition of gentility and order in his family background tells strongly in his thinking. From his earliest work, death has been present in one form or another. In an early woodcut, *Aspect of Point Lance*, he depicts a live tree and a dead one, mirroring, perhaps, some aspect of his own inner state at the time. He has watched the slow decay of the outports. When he was ten, his brother and only sibling was born, an experience that psychologists claim creates an acute sense of loss in older children. Pratt was thirteen when Newfoundland voted to join the Canadian Confederation. His family voted against it, almost en bloc, and the issue is still a contentious one that contributes to the tenuousness of Pratt's search for identity. The recovery of a lost identity in his paintings is a reflection of Pratt's own loss of and search for identity. His paintings of nudes are all, in one sense, a declaration of his identity as a professional artist working within the traditions of art, a substitute for the uncertainty of both his local and national traditions.

P ratt's awareness of death is constant but not morbid. For him, it is a state of completeness, the closing of a circle. Occasionally it is portrayed by subjects such as the lynx, an endangered species, or such as the vanishing of the fishing stages of *Sheds in Winter* (page 58), or it can be inherent, as in the houses of *Demolitions on the South Side* (page 45). In a painting like *Coley's Point* (page 103), the reference is veiled but felt. Coley's Point, overlooking Conception Bay near Bay Roberts, is the place where many of Pratt's ancestors are buried in the cemetery of St.

John the Evangelist. The painting is neither joyful nor solemn but holds out a slight feeling of melancholy. Needless to say, the building in the painting does not exist: it is a structure of the imagination, which represents the significance of Coley's Point to the artist.

An elegy not only laments but also celebrates what it depicts. This, too, is part of Pratt's statement as an artist, and it is revealed in two ways. The first is in the purity of the subjects he paints, their ideal wholeness and completeness. This chaste and undefiled world of Pratt's is also an intelligible and sensuous world, one that casts his figure paintings into a clearer context. *Demolitions on the South Side* became so purified in the course of its development that the final picture seems a portrait of something being constructed rather than being torn down. The clutter and disorder have been tidied away, and these ruins are new-minted epitaphs to what has been.

In his work, Pratt is asking us to try to find some validation of the present through contemplation and reflection. Pratt's art is an art of redemption from time because it reminds us that life is here and now, not there and then. It reminds us that the only value in knowing what has been is the significance it bestows on the present. In his images of man's monuments, time is breathlessly short; across the sea, it is eternal. These ideas, and the images that are inspired by them, reveal the contours of Pratt's mind, and he offers them to us as the most valid experiences of which he is capable. For, in a sense, Pratt's careful depiction has endowed the subjects that he paints with renewed life. The lost spirit is recovered in an enduring image, a lasting work of art, to celebrate both past and continuing life.

THE PLATES

I did several watercolours of St. John's during the winter of 1956. They were concerned with the look and feel of my birthplace, which yielded easily to techniques I had learned from reproduction of watercolours. Those same prototypes directed me toward the more picturesque, higgeldy-piggeldy aspects of that hillside, harbour town. Those preoccupations were short-lived: I had already done drawings and some gouache paintings of St. John's that were more concerned with structure and order. I still like those cold wet days and the northeast wind that assured me I was home.

South Side
1952
Gouache
8½″ x 6″
Collection the Artist

Battery Road
1956
Watercolour
15½″ x 19½″
Collection Mr. Dalton Robertson

The way I approach realism, my concern with form—in short, everything I know from an academic point of view—I either learned myself or learned in Glasgow. The back wall of the buildings across the lane from my flat was like an exhibition of windows. It always seemed to be grey and rainy, the kind of scene I had learned to paint back home. So I felt very easy with the subject. It was an opportunity to strut my stuff.

Glasgow Road
1958
Chalk and Charcoal on grey paper
12″ x 17¼″
Collection Mary Pratt

Grosvenor Crescent
1957
Watercolour
18½″ x 28⅜″
Collection Mary Pratt

Study for Haystacks
1960
Ink on paper
4½″ x 9″
Collection the Artist

Study for Haystacks
1960
Ink on paper
9″ x 23″
Collection the Artist

I took to silkscreen printing like the proverbial duck to water: I borrowed one of the art school's screens, stretched some silk and made my stencil, painting directly on the silk with glue. I still make my prints in this way; they are more like multiple paintings than conventional graphics. I remember the farms around St. John's when I was a boy, with shelters to keep the hay dry all winter—just a roof, the side of the stack functioning as its own thatch. But more than the subject matter, I was concerned with the design, with the pattern of the stubble and the haystacks and the light across the snow.

Haystacks in December
1960
Original signed screenprint,
edition of 7
11¼″ x 28″

This painting started as a rough pen sketch in which the buildings were seen from an angle. As I worked with the subject and developed it, it swung more and more to the front so that the façade became a series of right angles. It was the beginning of my preoccupation with frontality.

Study for Demolitions on the
South Side
1960
Ink on paper
5″ x 9″
Collection the Artist

Study for Demolitions on the
South Side
1960
Graphite on paper
5¼″ x 11″
Collection the Artist

Demolitions on the South Side
1960
Oil on canvas
17⅝″ x 39½″
Collection Dalhousie Art Gallery
Dalhousie University,
Halifax, Nova Scotia

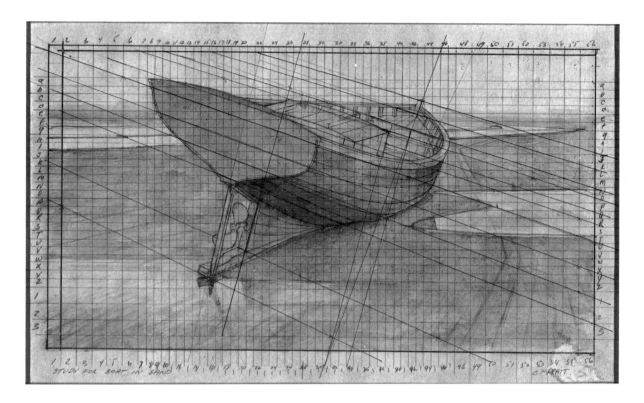

I have always loved boats. When I was a boy they were far more common, and far more important than cars. They said Newfoundland to me. I didn't intend this print as a symbol, but I did it at a time when it seemed to me that traditional and viable social structures were being systematically discredited in Newfoundland.

Study for Boat in Sand
1960
Graphite and watercolour on paper
5½″ x 9½″
Collection the Artist

Boat in Sand
1961
Original signed screenprint,
edition of 25
14″ x 26″

House and Barn
1962
Oil on board
15½″ x 35⅛″
Collection Canadian Department
of External Affairs

Once, at a very unhappy period in my life, I dreamed of moving to some remote head-land, of being able to see this kind of house out of my window: the archetypical house I've been painting ever since. The snow along the grass and the light coming from the same direction as the wind give a sense of move-ment and exposure, of the sweep of wind coming in off the sea. I sometimes use light as a metaphor for wind. The two things that made the strongest impression on me as a child were buildings or rooms and the sea.

Study for House and Barn
1962
Graphite on paper
4" x 9"
Collection the Artist

49

I wanted to pay homage to the lynx, a mysterious and cunning animal and one of the few indigenous to Newfoundland. (Perhaps hoping to possess some of its speed and daring, I once named a boat after it.) I used the barrens, with their distances and dwarf alder bushes, to add to the secretive, surrealistic quality. This is a rabbit's eye view of the lynx. It's last view, I imagine.

Boy with Rabbits
1965
Graphite on paper
4″ x 5¾″
Collection the Artist

The Lynx
1965
Original signed screenprint,
edition of 20
17″ x 29½″

It's easy to be anthropomorphic about windows; they lend human attributes to buildings: sight, dignity, mystery, transparency.

The origin of 'The Empty Room' was a house on Waterford Bridge Road, owned by a man who was blind. He had no curtains, no paintings, no decorations of any kind. And the mirror over the fireplace had been removed. As a child I found this very spooky: a house with nothing on the walls and yet inhabited.

Window by the Sea
1963
Graphite on paper
12″ x 7½″
Memorial University Art Gallery
St. John's, Newfoundland
Permanent Collection

The Empty Room
1964
Graphite on paper
13″ x 15″
Memorial University Art Gallery
St. John's, Newfoundland
Permanent Collection

I did not intend a lamentation, but the abandoned shops and the changes in the small communities I have lived in or visited filled me with nostalgia. More than a vanishing way of life, it is myself I mourn for: the loss of part of my identity. I'm curious about New-foundland's past, and proud of it. People who don't know where they've been or what they've been generally don't know where they're going or who they are. But at the same time I'm not so myopic as to believe that you can judge people by their past. I think you have to judge people by their aspirations.

Outport Business
1964
Watercolour
12⅞″ x 26¼″
Collection Vancouver Art Gallery
Vancouver, British Columbia

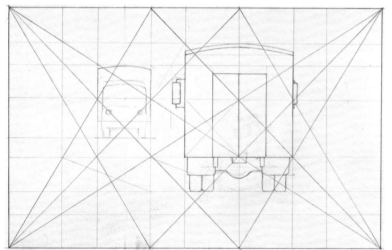

I am more concerned with potential than with reality. It's like throwing a ball in the air: physicists say there's a point, an instant, when it is frozen, neither going up nor coming down. Well, that's the moment I'm concerned with, the apex of the toss, when change is inevitable.

Pickup, Harricot Road
1965
Graphite on paper, unfinished
6″ x 12″
Collection the Artist

Study for Trucks Passing
1965
Graphite on paper
4″ x 6½″
Collection the Artist

Trucks Passing
1965
Graphite on paper
9″ x 14½″
Private Collection

Along the coast, fishermen used to hoist their catch straight out of the sea onto the cliffs, where the fish would be split, salted, and spread out to air-dry over the summer on platforms or flakes. This print is a souvenir of those fishing sheds. I remember their picturesque, lichen-patterned, work-stained walls and higgeldy-piggeldy look, but I eliminated most of that and emphasized the vertical and horizontal forms. What always struck me was the beauty of the engineering in those utilitarian structures.

Sheds in Winter
1964
Original signed screenprint,
edition of 25
14″ x 27⅞″

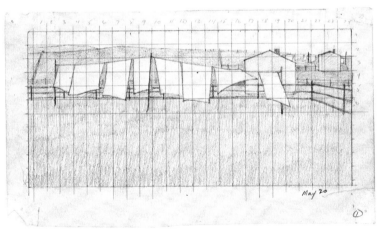

I use visual devices to describe other than visual dimensions, so the sheets hanging on the line convey the notion of not so much a breeze as a flow, a lift of sea air from the Cape Shore. I am aware that the sea is there behind the hill.

Study for Clothesline
1965
Graphite on paper
6" x 3"
Collection the Artist

Clothesline
1965
Original signed screenprint
and mixed media
12" x 26¾"
Collection Frank Ryan

59

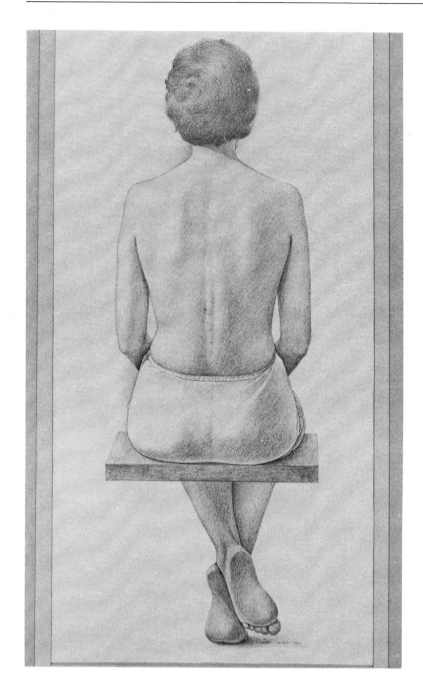

I invented everything in this painting, the room, the wallpaper, the dresser, even the figure; although, I did have a friend sit so I could check proportions. It is not a painting of an individual, but an environment which the person is part of. It is an environment for me, a sanctuary.

Woman Sitting (Study for
Woman at a Dresser)
Graphite on paper
20¼″ x 10½″
Collection Mrs. Sonia Dawe Ryan

Woman at a Dresser
1964
Oil on board
26″ x 30″
CIL Art Collection

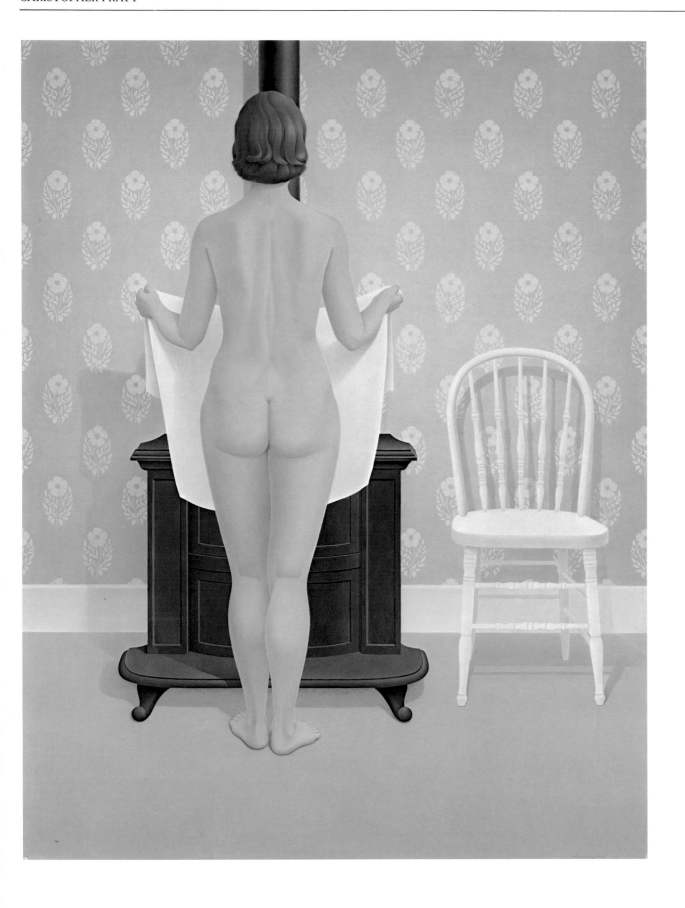

Woman and Stove
1965
Oil on board
30″ x 24″
Memorial University Art Gallery
St. John's, Newfoundland
Permanent Collection

I did not have much experience of the impersonal, professional-studio environment. I was interested in ordinary, domestic settings for my figures. My workroom has a Franklin stove, and we had a chair like that in our kitchen. I liked the contrast between the stove and the chair. I almost painted the figure out to concentrate on that.

Painting wallpaper is an excuse to paint flowers, which otherwise never enter into my work. I have only used wallpaper in the figure paintings; those rooms are softer, gentler, than the ones I imagine being alone in.

Young Woman Dressing
1966
Oil on board
37⅛″ x 21⅜″
Collection Mrs. Christine Pratt

I knew this model fairly well and I realized that her own bedroom wouldn't look like this, but as I drew her, we talked about things she liked and I imagined it this way. So the room, the light, and the things she is wearing are all a portrait of her. It is a real privilege, a luxury, to be able to work with girls who are not professional models. They have no preconceptions. It isn't really a studio relationship, an artist/model situation. They're just kids with their clothes off; the precedents they bring are from their own bedrooms.

Study for Young Woman
with a Slip
1967
Graphite on paper
21″ x 10″
Memorial University Art Gallery
St. John's, Newfoundland
Permanent Collection

Young Woman with a Slip
1967
Oil on board
33¾″ x 22½″
Collection Art Gallery
of Hamilton
Hamilton, Ontario
Gift of the Women's Committee
and Wintario, 1978

I remember the tranquillity of childhood afternoons, when the dishes were done and the men were still away from the house. More than the description of a kettle or a clock or a kitchen stove, this painting is about a mood and a time of day. I try to create rooms, both physical and philosophical, in which the mind can wander and play.

Three O'Clock
1968
Oil on board
15½″ x 18″
Collection Mr. and Mrs.
Irving Ungerman

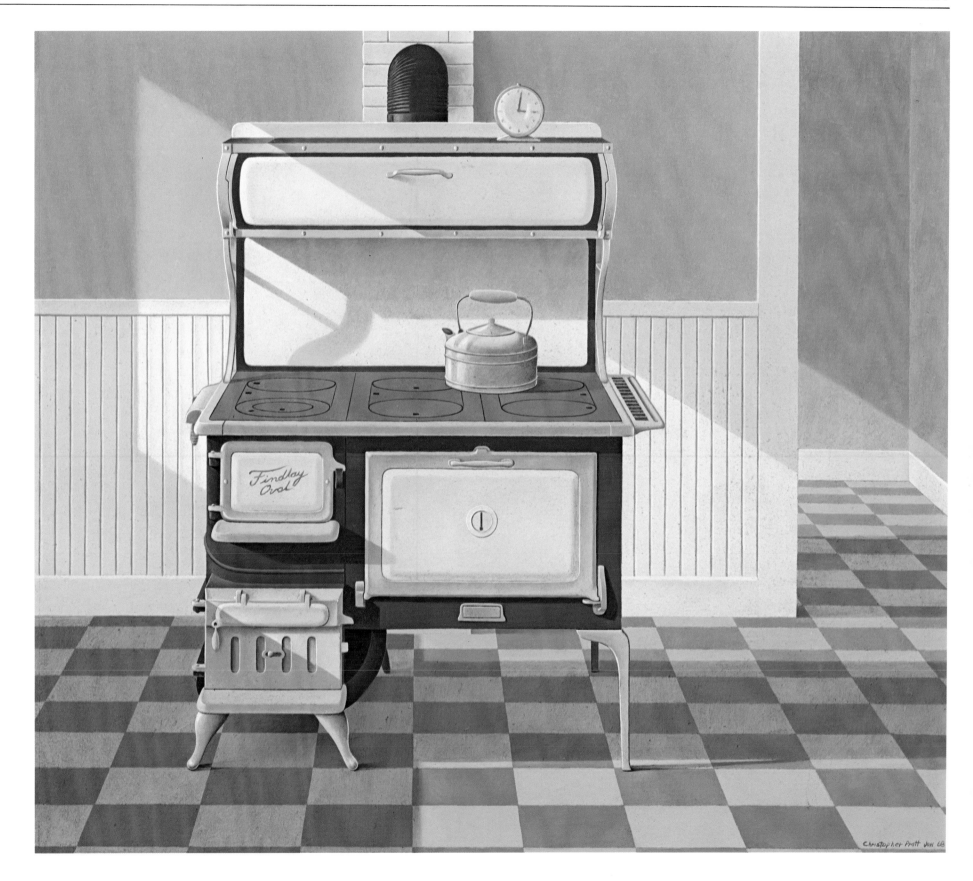

I made some sketches of a closed shop, which had windows crammed with all kinds of plants in old coffee cans and boilers. But the more I worked, the more specific I became. I try to avoid scenarios, so I removed the plants, pulled down the blinds and called it 'Shop on Sunday'. Then there was no way of telling whether it was closed for the day or closed forever. If art has any function at all, it's to provide launching pads for examination, for speculation, for an exercise of conscious awareness. Nothing pleases me more than the realization that people sense something in my paintings, but that they are not directed to what that something may be specifically. If ten different people tell me they see ten different things in a painting, then I think the painting is very successful.

Shop on Sunday
1968
Oil on board
11″ x 19″
Collection Canadian Department
of External Affairs

I drive the fifty-five miles to St. John's two or three times a week and often encounter a snow plough. It's a circular experience: the steering wheel and all the gauges, the sweep of the windshield wiper, the plough blowing snow across the road. I'm fascinated by big machines. It's amazing to watch them in operation. But the reason I haven't done much about them in my work is that I haven't had many first-hand encounters, they generally don't enter into my daily life.

Plough in a Storm
1967
Original signed screenprint,
edition of 25
19¼″ round

We often went trouting, in April and May, at the mouth of a brook or river where it entered the sea. That was different from fishing inland where the countryside was wild and tangled with black spruce and juniper, and where the trout came dark from the peat-stained water. Here everything was silver, bright; and there were measured fields and houses, often abandoned. I like the marks that cultivation leaves, evidence of mankind where our presence is benign. I like places that are open, bare, exposed, where the air is so clean I can taste it and where the light is carried on the saltspray wind, bleaching and illuminating. That's Newfoundland in the spring for me.

Two Houses in the Spring
1968
Original signed screenprint,
edition of 25
10¾″ x 29″

This was a sensuous little exercise, done at a time when I was experimenting with ink on paper prepared with gelatin and chalk. I had taken the egg out of the fridge with the intention of extending this experiment into egg tempera. I wound up drawing the egg instead. I have never done a full, egg tempera painting.

When we first came to St. Mary's Bay there were frequent power failures; I remember one that lasted four days. Our kerosene lamps weren't just ornaments, souvenirs from the romantic past. Lamplight has an area; you can see its edge against the darkness.

An Egg
1967
Ink and opaque white
on gesso wash
4½" x 3½"
Collection Leda Bell

Lamp in a Window
1968
Ink and opaque white
on gesso wash
8⅝" x 10"
Private Collection

I am genuinely moved by buildings, by the windows and rooms and shelters made by man. That interest in architecture precedes the composition and design: starting as a back view, with a cellar door, uneven blinds, and a chimney to one side, this house resolved itself into an austere, symmetrical view from the front. I even omitted the doorknob because it would have violated the symmetry. When people say, as some have, that there's very little humanity in my work, I don't know quite how to answer them, except that they may be mistaking my intentions. When I'm working well I get a particular feedback from what I'm doing, and what I get is a sense of a kind of person, a sense of a kind of place, a sense of a kind of situation. And, although it sounds banal and trite to say it, I get a sense of myself. Because the whole process is, as it were, an act of research into one's own humanity. That's what I think the creative process is. You are researching a humanity, and the only humanity you have access to is your own.

House in August
1968
Interim State

House in August
1969
Oil on board
17½″ x 24½″
Collection Mr. and Mrs. W. Teron

I use light to render form on a two-dimensional surface. I think of it as an illumination, an atmosphere, a presence of weight: as something physical. It is a tool of illusion. I am more concerned with volume than texture, with the boat as a cup, a vessel.

Gregory's Punt
1969
Ink on gesso wash
9" x 17"
Collection David P. Silcox

Coal and Salt
1970
Ink and watercolour on gelatin
and chalk wash
16½″ x 29″
Collection Mrs. Joan Irving

Initially, I was just drawing a shed: the crisp pattern of the wall, the heavier concrete underneath, and the texture of the rubble. Extremities always appeal to me. As I worked, I kept thinking of coal; my grandfather and, subsequently, my mother and her brothers were in the coal and salt business. Then I began to be aware of a coincidence, of a parallel between the qualities of coal and salt —one, heavy and opaque; the other, crystalline, transparent, soluble—and between the mat, black ink, and shiny paper, prepared with a coat of gelatin and chalk so it had a light, granular surface, like a salt lick. In the end, I decided to add some letters, so with great delight I painted Dawe, my mother's maiden name, on the door.

Shed Door
1968
Ink and watercolour on gesso wash
12″ x 12″
Collection Richard and
Sandra Gwyn

*I have often wondered why people paint
symbols on barn doors. Is it to protect the
animals, or to protect themselves from the
animals? Has it got something to do with
Christ's birth in a stable? Whatever the reason
may be, I think it's a good idea: a wise
precaution.*

Barn and Cellar
1969
Oil on board
16⅜″ x 40⅝″
Private Collection

An expanse of sky and water represents an expanse of time to me. Also, the sky and ice and water are primarily geophysical elements (whereas trees and grass are organic). I see the universe as a geophysical entity in which the biological is rare.

Ice
1972
Collage
12″ x 12″
Collection David P. Silcox

Ice
1972
Original signed screenprint,
edition of 30
18″ x 18″

83

The Strait of Belle Isle is the only place where one can see the continent of North America from the island of Newfoundland, where one gets that wonderful, offshore feeling, and knows that this land has a definition more natural, more precise than arbitrary longitudes or parallels: the meeting, all around, of land and sea. In the winter, great wild places like the Strait of Belle Isle come into their own. Off-season, they regain their privacy and dignity.

Strait of Belle Isle
1972
Original signed screenprint,
edition of 30
18″ x 18″

The very word 'Labrador' was magic to me when I was a child. That was before the Churchill Falls development or the iron mines. The tales I heard were of the coast, of heroism and hardship, of nature on a giant scale; a land where the fish were bigger, the icebergs massive, the storms unimaginable. Somehow, I felt that Newfoundland was the child of Labrador—the tail that wagged the dog. In geographical terms that is certainly true: here in St. Mary's Bay we live at a latitude south of Vancouver, yet we have plants and animals in common with the Arctic tundra. The Labrador current is a relentless flood of molten ice, the blood stream of our near sub-Arctic climate.

Labrador Current
1973
Collage
12″ x 12″
Collection David P. Silcox

Labrador Current
1973
Original signed screenprint,
edition of 25
18″ x 18″

87

I have lived in two houses that were built into hills, so that one wall was underground. The windows opposite had the effect of a cave opening. Men used to live in caves: ordinary men, then holy men, whose shelters now are shrines. That inside/outside contrast is in a lot of my work. I am fascinated with the many places in Newfoundland that have been abandoned, standing empty and cavelike as if something has frightened or spirited everyone away.

Shop on an Island
1969
Oil on board
32″ x 36″
Collection London Regional
Art Gallery
London, Ontario
Gift of Mr. J. H. Moore
Through the Ontario
Heritage Foundation

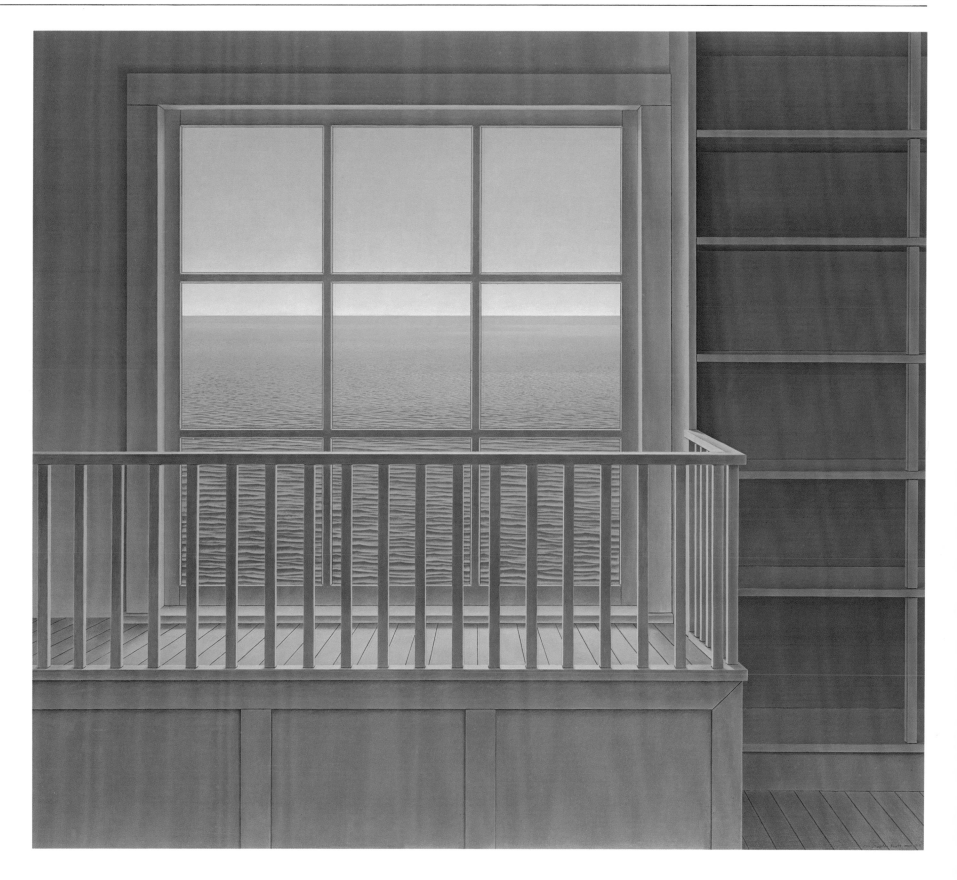

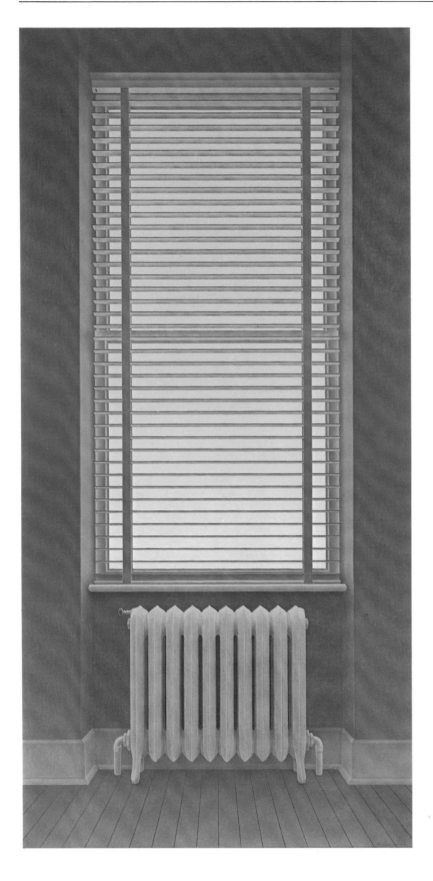

Once, I woke up in a Prince Edward Island hotel room in a bed so low all I could see was the sky. What ultimately interested me were the abstract elements: the staccato change in width and visual weight of the Venetian blind slats in response to perspective, against the more subtle and organic change in the sky from blue to paler pink, and the further contrast of the heavy verticals of the old-fashioned iron radiator. This painting was an incredible labour; you need a steady hand for horizontals.

Window with a Blind
1970
Oil on board
48″ x 24″
Collection Norcen Energy
Resources Limited

There's something church-like about walking up a dark stairway and coming into the light. I recall (I was twelve or thirteen, living on Waterford Bridge Road in St. John's) the window on the stairway landing of a friend's house, where the light shone through bright, coloured glass. I tend to understate, so I didn't emphasize the colour.

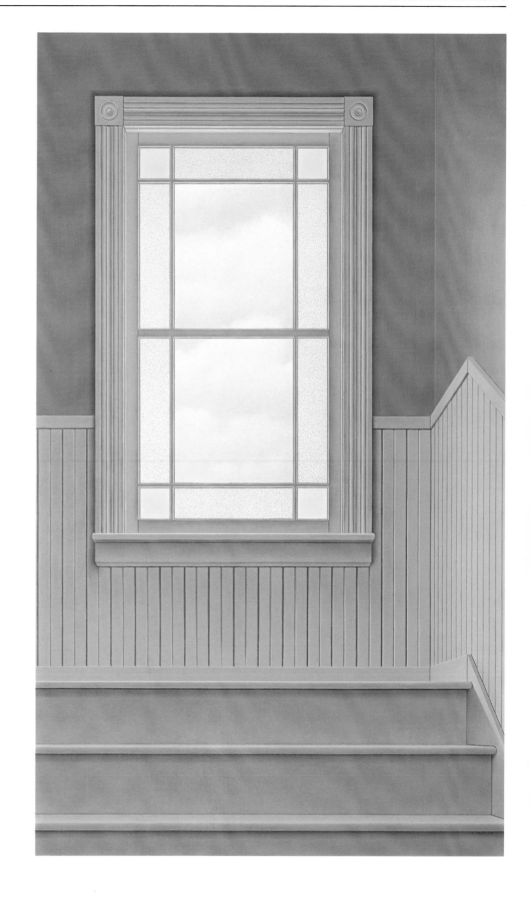

Window on the Stairs
1969
Oil on board
40" x 24"
Collection Vancouver Art Gallery
Vancouver, British Columbia

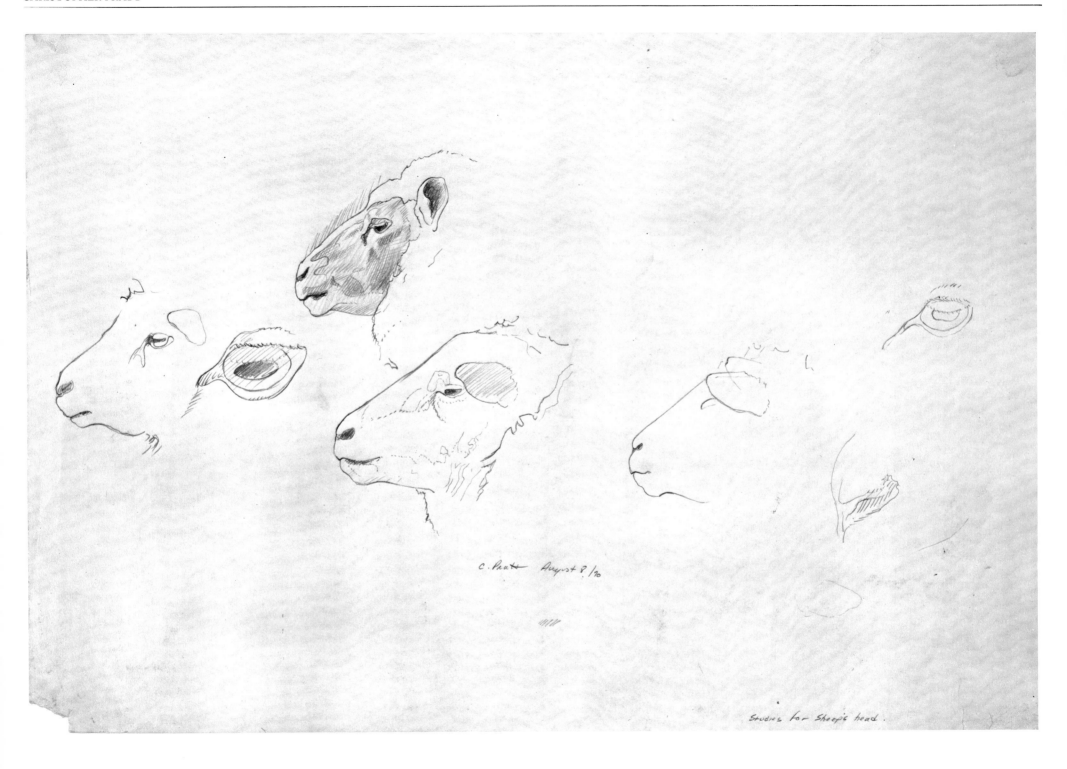

Sheet of studies for Sheep
1971
Graphite on paper
12″ x 18″
Collection the Artist

*I don't come to animal subjects easily but I
wanted to do a sheep, because for me, sheep
epitomize St. Mary's Bay. I made several
drawings, including one of a sheep lying in
a shed with neon eyes glowing in the dark, but
in the end, I shied away from the melodrama.
Technically, this was one of the most frus-
trating prints I ever did: so many little dots.
I worked on it for four months.*

The Sheep
1971
Original signed screenprint,
edition of 25
13⅝″ x 31″

A nicely made bed is ambiguous: in a neat, hospital-like room, it is impossible to tell if the owner has gone to work for the day, has gone away for a month, or is dead, gone forever. Colour is intuitive, a potent device to establish mood. I associate pink with blood, not blood red as in a rose, but blood that is dried and pale and spent. Like 'Good Friday', this is an Easter image.

Study for The Bed
1971
Graphite and watercolour wash
on paper
13″ x 15″
Collection Mira Godard

The Bed
1971
Oil on board
34″ x 27¼″
Beaverbrook Art Gallery
Fredericton, New Brunswick
Wallace S. Bird Memorial
Collection
Gift of the Beaverbrook
Canadian Foundation

95

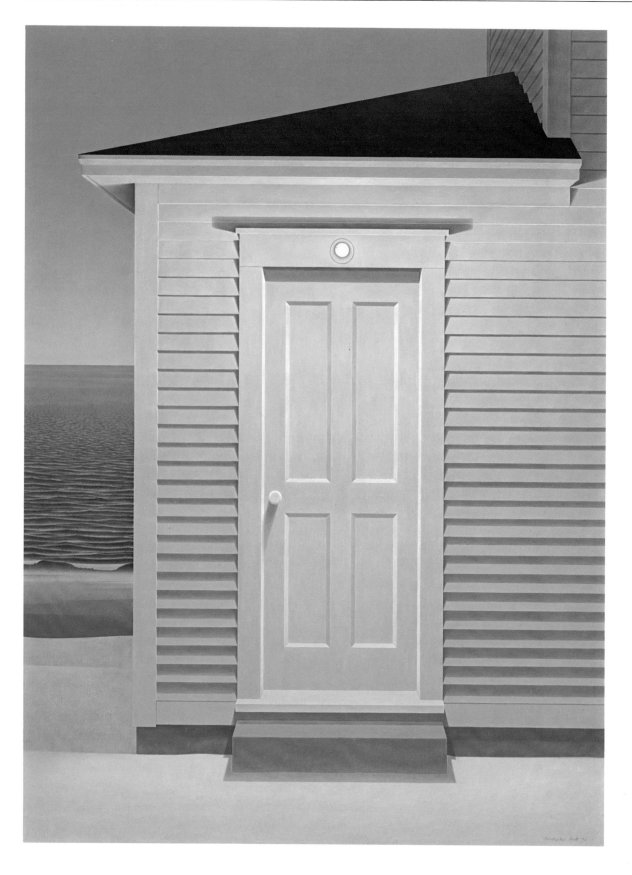

There's a welcoming quality to a light and to a porch door. I like that time of day when it is light, yet dark, because you get a beautiful juxtaposition between an artificially illuminated house, with its deepening bands of shadows, and the residual daylight, the sky a smooth blend from garish blue to sunset orange.

It was a bright warm day and the lighthouse tower glistened like a pillar of salt. Inside, it was cool and almost black. It was a strange door that led into the darkness of a light.

Porch Light
1972
Oil on board
31⅞" x 23⅝"
Collection Mrs. Christine Pratt

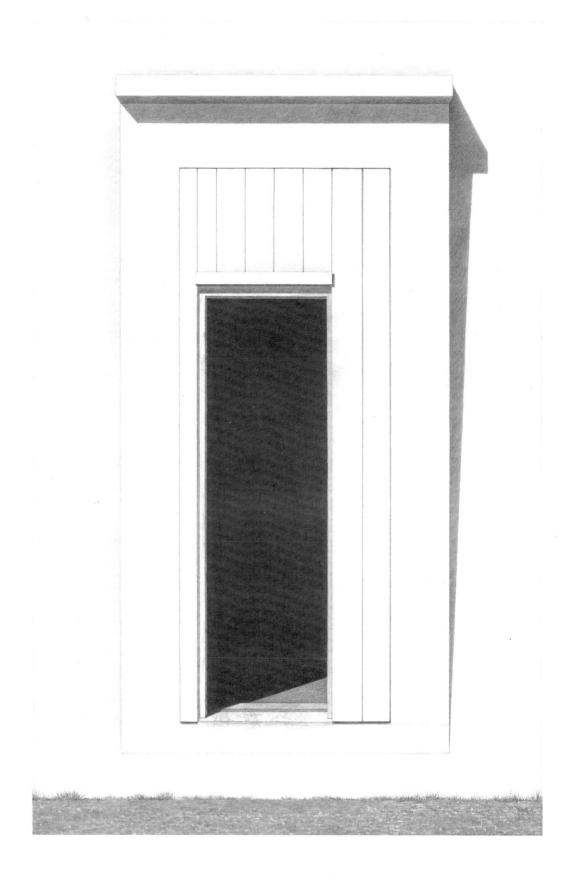

Lighthouse Door
1972
Graphite on paper
17″ x 11″
Collection Mira Godard Gallery

I was intrigued by the juxtaposition of that fresh, optimistic blue with the total pessimism of the environment: the drab brown and dirty cream, the night window reflecting the dusty wall of the waiting room. I find waiting for a train, or for anything, to be demeaning. Stations remind me that we're all powerless and ordinary. I don't want to be subject to anyone else's schedule. I crave to be in control.

Study for Station
1972
Graphite and crayon on paper
5½″ x 9″
Collection the Artist

Study for Station
1972
Graphite on paper
4″ x 6½″
Collection the Artist

Station
1972
Oil on board
33½″ x 54⅜″
Collection Confederation Centre
Art Gallery and Museum,
Charlottetown,
Prince Edward Island

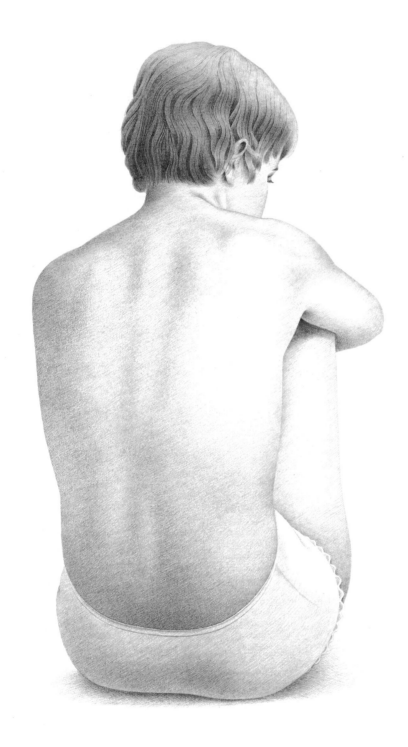

She was a very private, self-contained, delicate, young girl. She liked to pose, but she instinctively turned away, sheltered herself. She sat there preoccupied with something else, as if being in the studio was like sitting on a hilltop on a warm, soft day.

Girl Sitting
1972
Graphite on paper
15″ x 10″
Private Collection

Girl Looking in a Mirror
1972
Graphite on paper
8″ x 8″
Private Collection

*I liked the shapes in her back as she was
undressing so I said, 'Hold it like that.'
Of course, you can't 'hold it'; movement is
more than an infinite number of static points.*

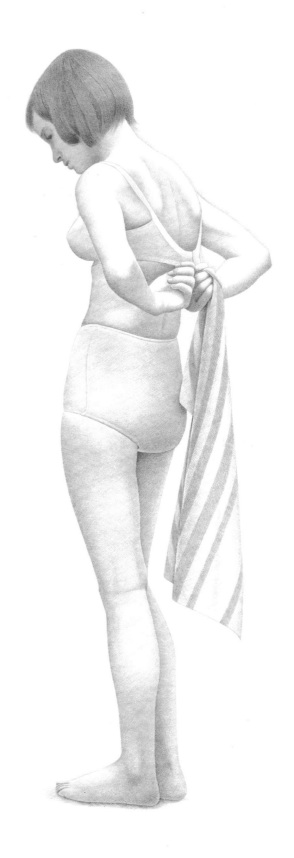

Girl with a Striped Towel
1972
Graphite on paper
21″ x 10½″
Private Collection

I have a preoccupation with the space-equals-time equation and with the juxtaposition of near and far. I like the definitions and arrangements here: the visual infinity of the sea foiled by the frontal, shallow space of the window, the fine verticals of the fence, and the heavy horizontals of shadows under clapboard. When I finished the print, there was a kind of quiet which suggested the title.

Sunday Afternoon
1972
Original signed screenprint,
edition of 30
16½" x 28"

My grandparents, great-grandparents, and umpteen aunts and uncles are buried in the cemetery at Coley's Point. Originally, the door was a coffin image: the proportions, first of all, and then the oval, urn-like window. I was going to use hardwood, stained and varnished to look like mahogany, and a small, glass nameplate with my mother's family name in silver. In the end, I took the nameplate off and painted the door. The image turned out much more dispassionate than it started. Sometimes I find things too strong for me and I back away.

Coley's Point
1973
Oil on board
26″ x 42″
Private Collection

Study for Institution
1973
Graphite on paper
4″ x 2½″
Collection the Artist

Study for Institution
1973
Graphite on paper
10¾″ x 6½″
Collection the Artist

Studies for Institution
1973
Graphite on paper
6½″ x 6½″
Collection the Artist

105

I'm fascinated by the architecture and impersonality of institutions. It may be a love/hate relationship. Once, when Mary was in the hospital, I jotted down in my five-and-dime diary: 'I do not feel the loathing for this room that I should. In fact, it's like one of my paintings: crisp, bare walls; the clean, efficient meeting of horizontals and verticals; an interesting play of tones from surface to surface. No cracks or irregularities where the dirt can hide. Have I been painting hospitals all my life?' I was turning the word 'institution' over in my mind and I started making sketches. I was inside, looking out. After several drawings I realized that what was emerging was a recollection of what I could see from a hospital bed once, when I was a boy. I enjoyed painting the steam. It was an escape from the impersonality of the other elements in the painting.

Study for Institution
1973
Graphite on paper
7½" x 7½"
Collection the Artist

Institution
1973
Oil on board
30″ x 30″
Collection National Gallery
of Canada
Ottawa, Ontario

107

When I look over the expanse of the Atlantic
at the rise and fall of great, soft swells made
palpable by the wind, I am always struck by
the extraordinary flatness of the sea. I like
flat places, the prairies, the Tantramar
Marshes, the barrens, deserts. Nearly everyone
associates open space with freedom. It's a
space where body, mind and soul might
wander endlessly, productively.

Study for Bay-2
1972
Collage
10¾″ x 22¼″
Collection David P. Silcox

Bay
1972
Oil on board
31⅜″ x 70½″
Private Collection
Edmonton, Alberta

I spent many Easter Holidays at my aunt's house in Bay Roberts. I associate Good Friday with the way the fields and houses looked at that time of year: pale, spent, everything exposed and vulnerable. I started with the title, so this print grew out of those associations. Winter was more comforting than spring: we had trees to cut for Christmas, but Easter lilies were from another part of the world.

Good Friday
1973
Original signed screenprint,
edition of 35
20″ x 22⅞″

French Door
1973
Oil on board
32″ x 32⅜″
Private Collection

Landing
1973
Oil on board
30″ x 38″
Private Collection

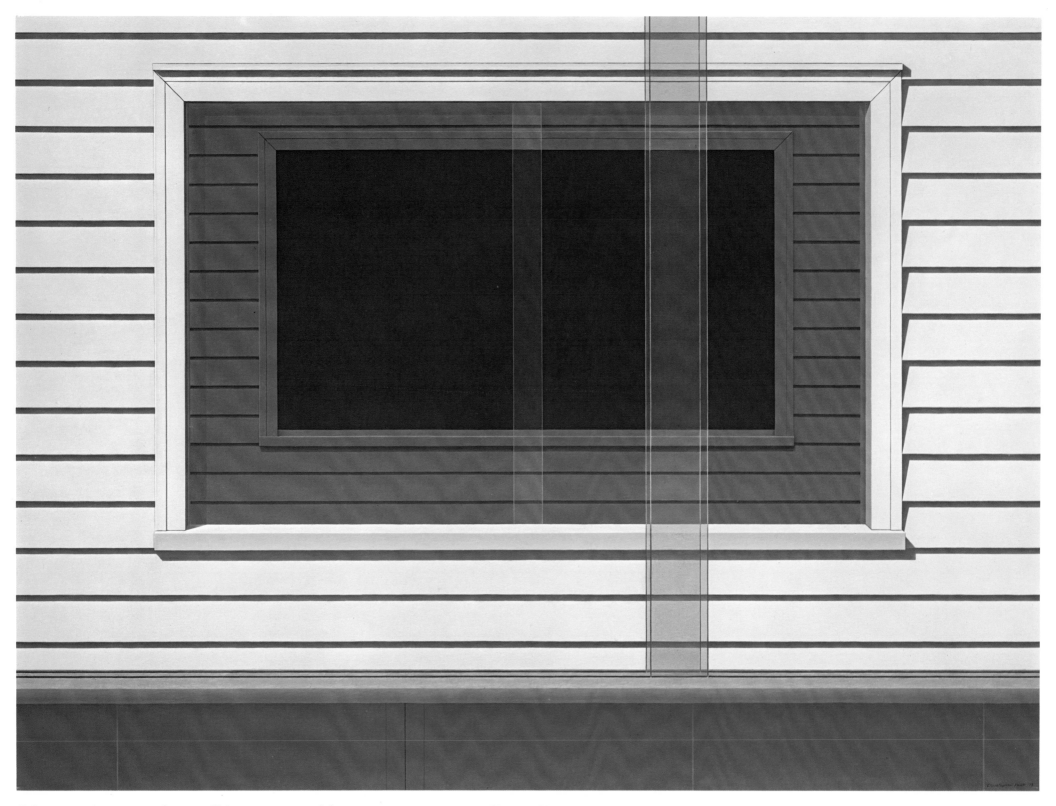

My own house is basically two, joined by a kitchen; it's really like living in a subdivision. The title is a play on the pattern, the potentially endless reflection that subdivides the painting, and on the endless repetition and up-close neighbourliness in a subdivision.

Subdivision
1973
Oil on board
25⅝" x 35½"
Collection Canada Council
Art Bank

In Newfoundland, the blinds are often drawn to keep sunlight from fading the furniture, but particularly when I was a boy, drawing the front room blinds was also a sign that someone had died. I wasn't trying to comment on either extreme: I like ambiguity.

Front Room
1974
Original signed screenprint,
edition of 35
23″ x 20″

115

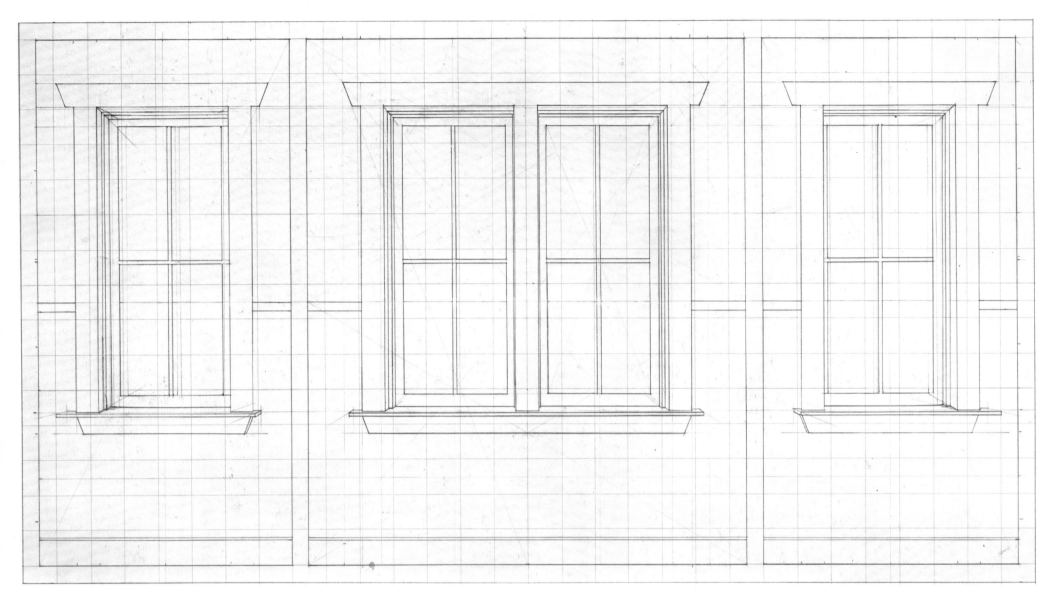

I chose the triptych device (the middle panel represents a fragment of the end wall; the side panels, side walls) to give the impression of multiplicity, of an endless group of identical windows. When you look out, you see the loom of land, underneath a fogbank. This is a village image, simple, parochial, a bit hide-bound. I don't think the religious experience in a parish hall has much to do with metaphysical infinity.

Study for Parish Hall
1974
Graphite on paper
8″ x 15″
Collection the Artist

Parish Hall
1974
Oil on board
31½″ x 59¾″
Private Collection

Study for Sails
1974
Graphite and crayon on paper
6″ x 9⅜″
Collection the Artist

Study for Ocean Racer
1975
Collage
6″ x 7″
Collection the Artist

Study for Ocean Racer
1975
Collage
6½″ x 9⅜″
Collection the Artist

118

Ocean Racer
1975
Original signed screenprint,
edition of 50
15″ x 24¼″

*Sailing on the ocean is an awe-inspiring
experience; you sense the roundness of the
world, feel open to the universe, unsheltered.
It conditions your understanding of everything.
The boat is an island on the sea with its
onboard life-support systems, just as our planet
is in space. Ocean racing as a sport is
unmatched in its scale and complexity.*

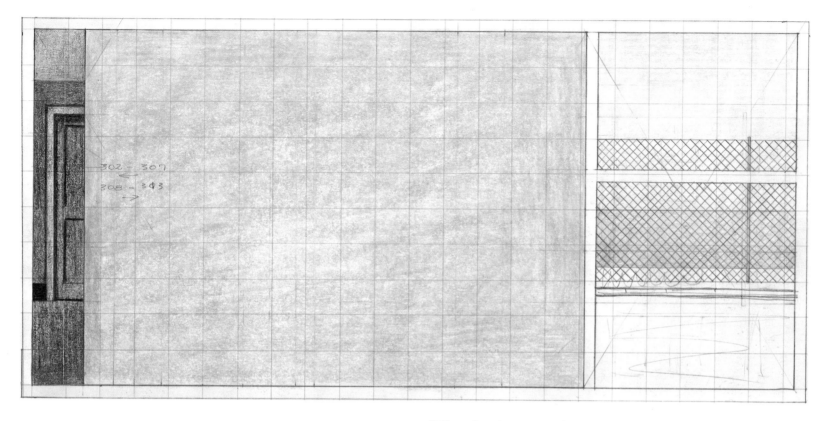

The drafting and surveying techniques I learned while studying engineering are still evident in the design and physical balance of my work: for me, painting is essentially a two-dimensional business. The architectural subject matter with its straight lines relates to organization and control and the presence of man; even my landscapes have long horizons, the ultimate straight line in nature.

Study for Federal Area
1975
Graphite and crayon on paper
5¼″ x 11½″
Collection the Artist

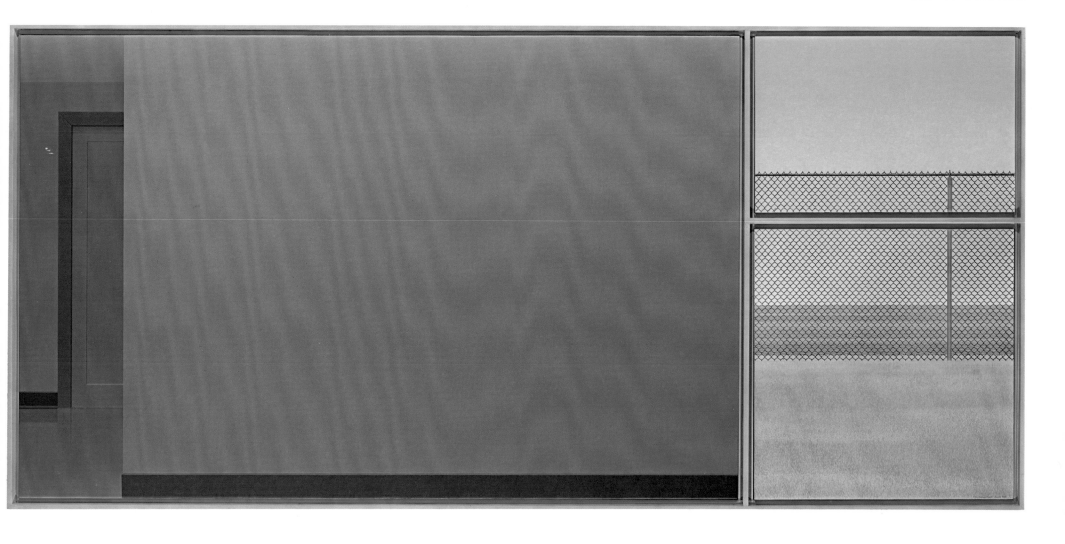

Federal Area
1975
Oil on board
31½″ x 68⅜″
Collection Mr. and Mrs. J. Lazare

Miss Power
1973
Graphite on paper
10¼″ x 13¼″
Collection Mira Godard Gallery

Girl with Nothing On
1981
Graphite on paper
12¾″ x 14¾″
Private Collection

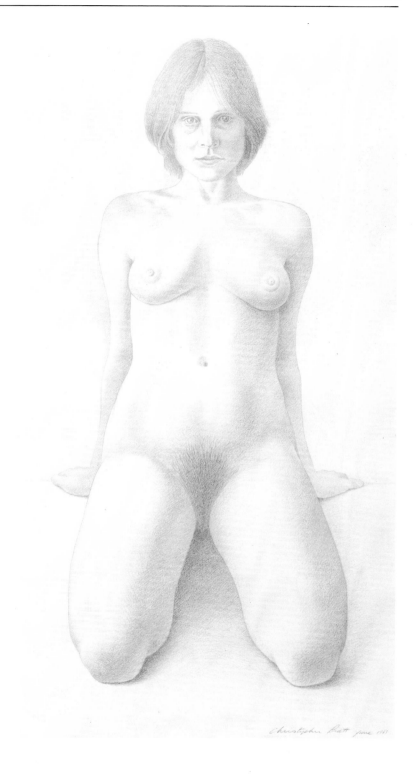

Madonna
1981
Graphite on paper
18″ x 10″
Collection Mira Godard

My work balances between representational and abstract. I always gravitate back to the kind of statement that hangs its hat on definition; although, above and beyond the physical, there is always some meaning. Art is not reality. The imitation of reality does not interest me. My trade is making images, strong images.

Donna (Study for Apartment)
1975
Graphite on paper
11½″ x 5¼″
Collection John and Margo Green

Apartment
1976
Oil on board
29½″ x 48″
Collection George Gardiner

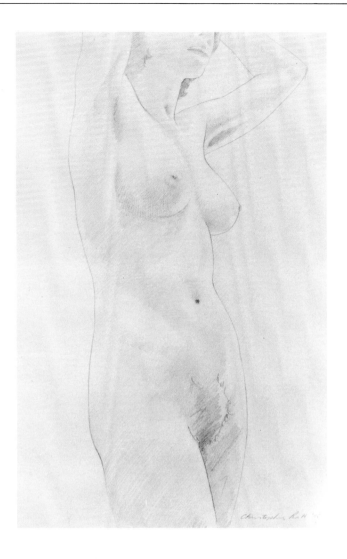

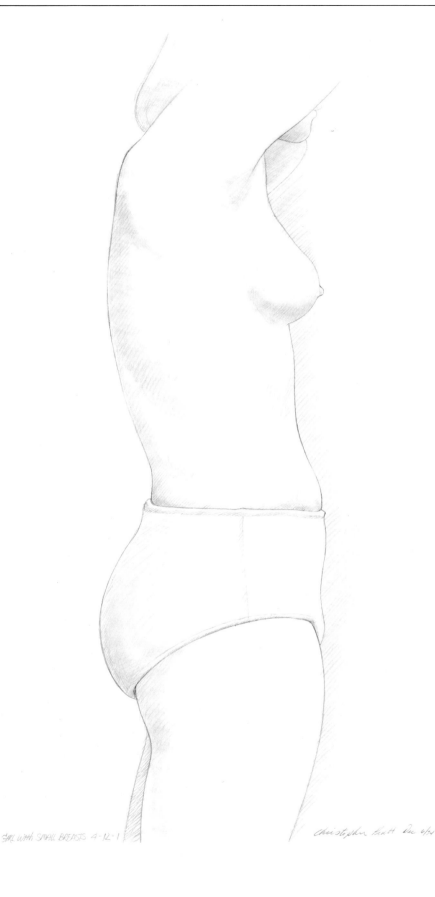

You can't ignore the individuality of people or overlook the details that identify their separateness as arrogantly as you can ignore irregularities that make a wall or room particular. Almost the only time I draw actual things, the way they are, is when I do preliminary figure work. (She didn't like the title.)

Girl with Small Breasts
1974
Graphite on paper
14″ x 8″
Private Collection

Nude with Raised Arms
1975
Graphite on paper
11″ x 17″
Private Collection

NUDE AND STUDIES

*I don't often sketch. Sketching requires a kind
of detachment that does not come easily to me,
so I usually draw, which is a more direct
and concentrated thing. When I do relax and
sketch, it's a real busman's holiday, then the
surface feel of things, textures, and irregularities interest me.*

Nude and Studies
1974
Graphite on paper
11″ x 19¼″
Collection Manuge Galleries
Limited

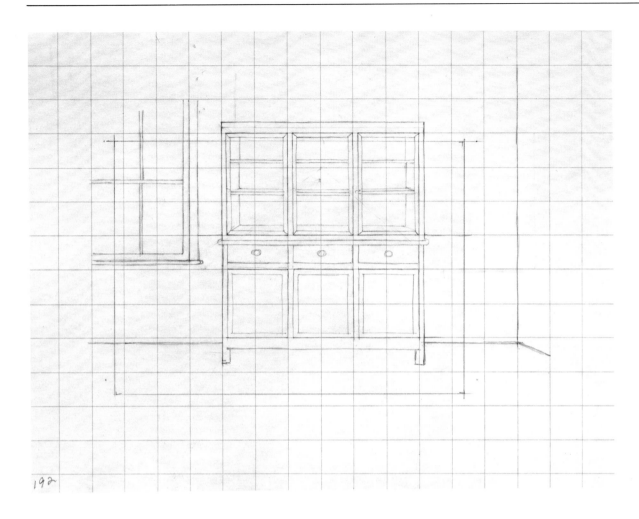

A few months ago, walking down a street in St. John's, I noticed a 'for sale' sign on the house I lived in as a child. I looked in, the first time I'd looked in that house since I was seven. It was incredible, the things there that have shown up in my paintings, obviously etched in my memory: windows and French doors, a fireplace, and a cupboard, almost identical to this one—identical, if you accept the abstractions that I use.

Study for Cupboard
1975
Graphite on paper
7″ x 9″
Collection the Artist

Cupboard
1975
Oil on board
26″ x 42″
Private Collection

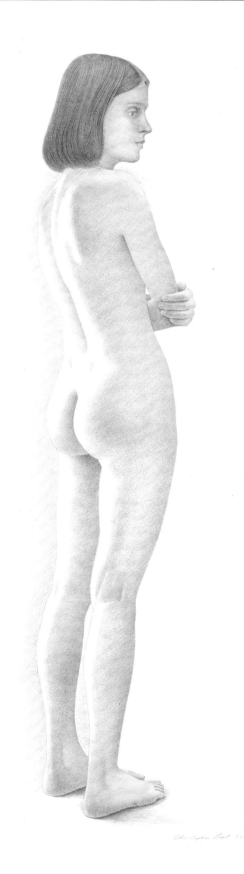

Donna was standing looking at a drawing I had started of her, which I abandoned there and then because this 'pose' was so much better. Most people who draw from life will tell you that the best poses happen when the model isn't posing at all. I started the drawing in May and I worked on it off and on for nearly a year. It seemed to me Donna changed a lot over that period of time.

This is a true-to-life drawing of a friend of ours. I only drew her once. She was much bigger physically and infinitely more confident and matter of fact than most of my models. She came from my own world.

Donna Last May
1976
Graphite on paper
21¼″ x 9″
Collection Mira Godard

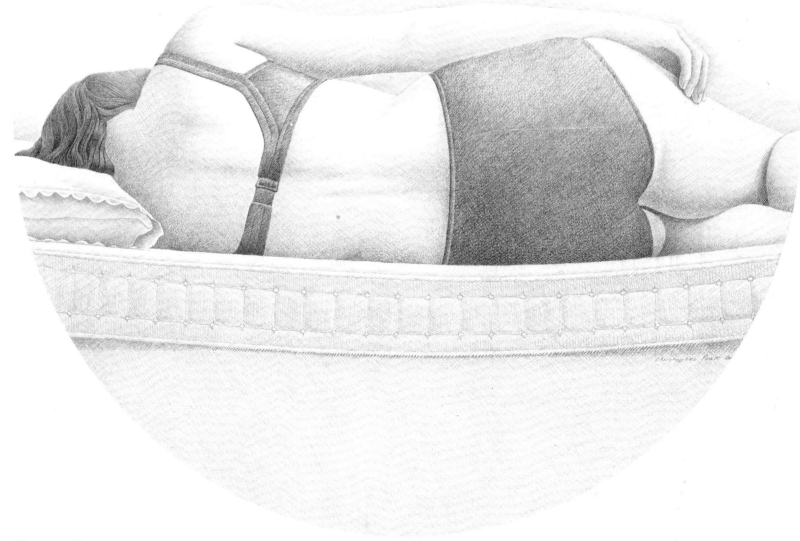

Woman in Black
1971
Graphite on paper
14¼″ round
Collection Edgar Davidson

Cape St. Mary's
1975
Original signed screenprint,
edition of 45
18" round

This print has less to do with sailing than with newness, that moment of possession: the boat—sleek, ruthless, and efficient, like a shark—hanging in the straps, ready to be lowered into the sea.

New Boat
1975
Original signed screenprint,
edition of 55
14½″ x 30″

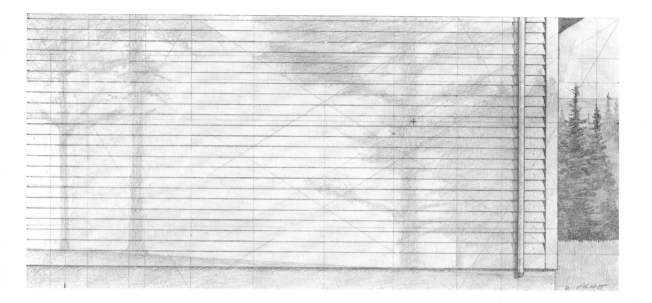

Spring at My Place
1976
Graphite and coloured pencil
on paper
4" x 9"
Collection the Artist

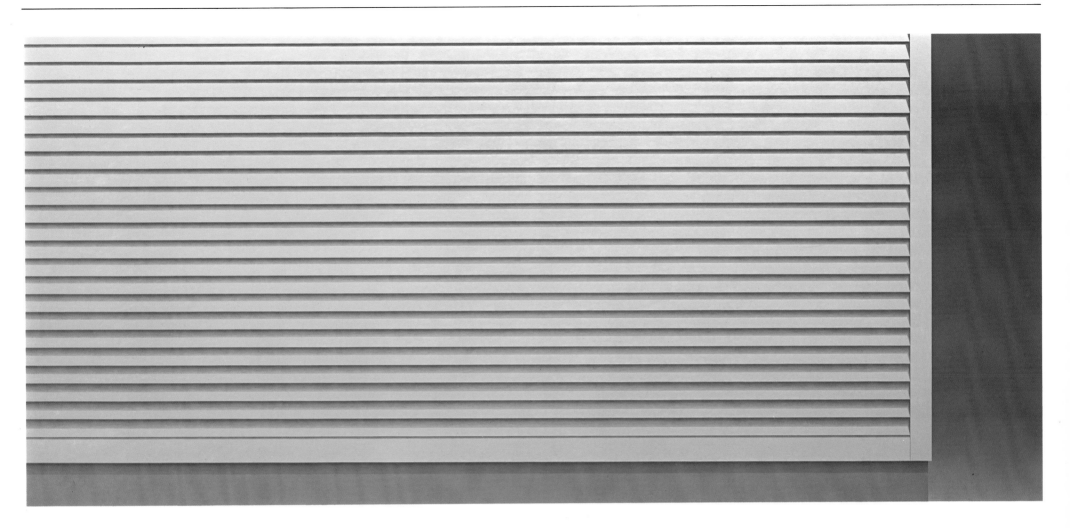

I like the immediacy, the sense of confrontation, between the wall of my house, with its gradation of shadow lines cast by the glow of a street light, and that indeterminate space, the darkness and mist and wild country across the river. I was working on this painting at a time of apprehension.

March Night
1976
Oil on board
40″ x 90″
Collection Art Gallery of Ontario
Toronto, Ontario
Purchased with assistance from
Wintario, 1977

This work relates to the passages I have made by sailboat from Lake Ontario through the Seaway and across the Gulf of St. Lawrence to Newfoundland. The slow, relentless, passage of the lakers summed up Lake Ontario for me. This is the first time I tried to print a blended sky. The experiment cost me dearly in ruined examples, and consequently, the print is in a relatively short edition of 35. There is considerable variety among those prints selected to make up this edition, far more variety than is usual in my editions. I consider that this variety was inevitable in the circumstances in which I made these prints — the limitations of my rather basic equipment — and not, therefore, a negative aspect. My main concern in picking an edition was that each individual print should stand on its own.

Lake Ontario
1976
Original signed screenprint,
edition of 35
20″ round

The breakwater at Long Pond, where I keep my boat, is extraordinarily regular with vertical piling and horizontal bracing. This print comes close to being a description of an actual place, and I have to credit my son Ned with bringing it to my attention. As a child he did a drawing of the wharf and light, a memory of many afternoons, and that drawing became my preliminary work. I like the pattern, the structure, the weight of the sky above.

Breakwater
1976
Original signed screenprint,
edition of 55
20″ x 28″

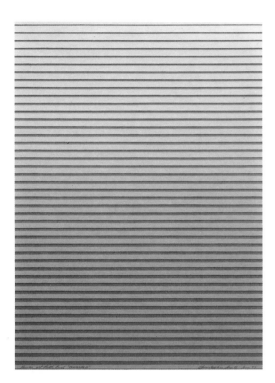

There is a community in St. Mary's Bay called Path End and presumably a similar house. But the title, with its trail's end overtone, came because it seemed to relate to the mood of the print or maybe to the mood I was in at the time. The last few years have forced me to come to grips with death. Exposing one's inner self through art is not easy. If you are a painter or a poet you sort of undress and go for a walk in the village square, so to speak, and you say 'this is me'. But then I suppose painters and poets are fascinated by that kind of revelation or they would do something else. You know, there's other work available.

The House at Path End-Clapboard
1977
Original signed screenprint,
unique
15″ x 10¾″

Collection David P. Silcox

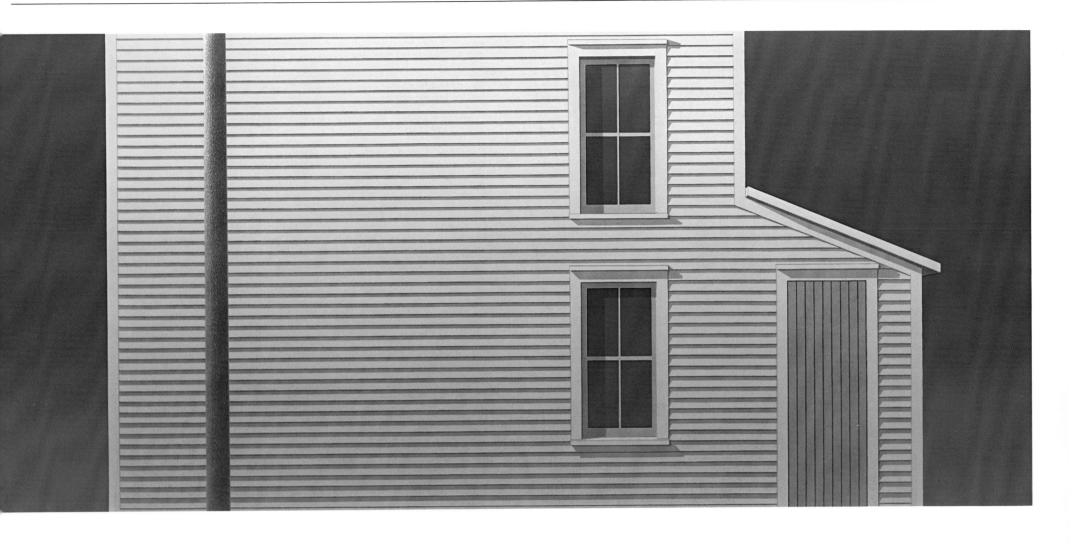

The House at Path End
1977
Original signed screenprint,
edition of 55
15″ x 33½″

Studies for The Visitor
1977
Graphite on paper
5½″ x 4½″
Collection the Artist

142

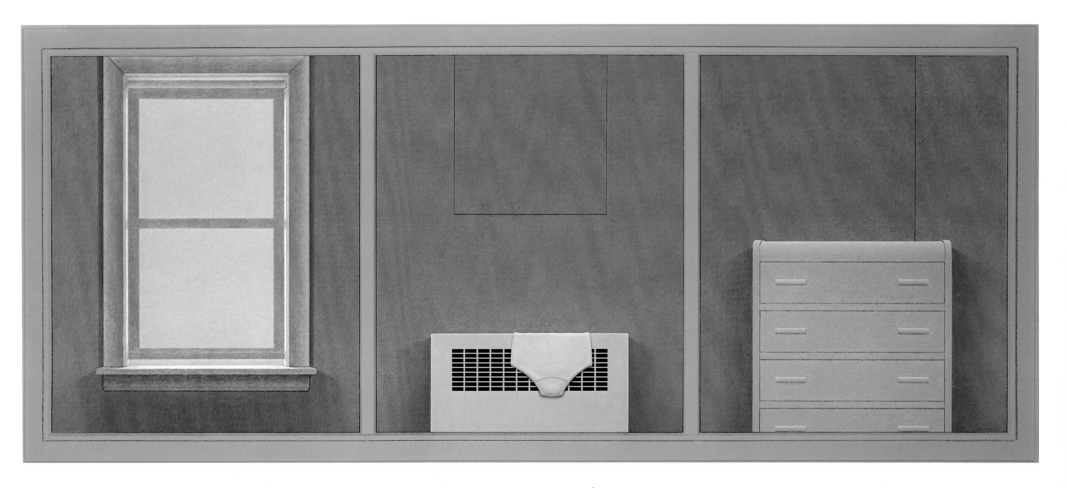

This image grew out of my experiences of being ensconced in a guest room. There's anonymity, mystery, and a kind of expectation when you settle down at night surrounded by drawn blinds and strange furniture. The underwear goes back to the notion of looking in cupboards or drawers—perhaps for a place to put your socks—and finding evidence of other people, finding things you really have no right to encounter: maybe just a hidden ornament or magazines they don't care to let you know they read.

The Visitor
1977
Oil on board
37⅛″ x 89″
Collection National Gallery
of Canada
Ottawa, Ontario

Summer Place
1975/78
Oil on board
23⅜″ x 25¼″
Collection Mira Godard

144

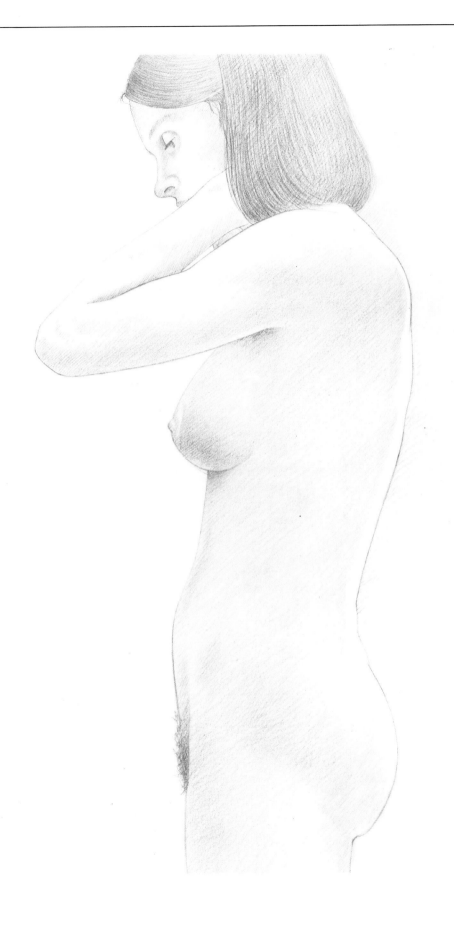

Girl Washing (Study for
Summer Place)
1976
Graphite on paper
12½″ x 13″
Collection Dr. and Mrs.
John Murray

145

On the Cape Shore, you can look across a crevice to another cliff, aware of the danger of falling down into the sea, but there is also a weird feeling that you could fall horizontally as well. I added the crow and raven to the patterns of snow and rock to establish that sense of horizontal space. Ravens are usually considered birds of ill-omen but I admire them. They're alive and functioning in landscapes where there's little other life. 'Crow and Raven' is outside the mainstream of my prints. There's something a little more picturesque in it. Something that I don't allow in most of my work. The original drawing of the cliffs was down on the Cape Shore, and some romantic aspects crept in as I was doing the print. I excused these because I was thinking about a friend who had just died and I knew he would like it that way, especially with the birds in it. He was some-one who liked the out-of-doors and natural things. It was a print he would have approved of, though it wasn't a memorial, properly speaking.

Crow and Raven
1978
Original signed screenprint,
edition of 45
16″ x 23⅞″

147

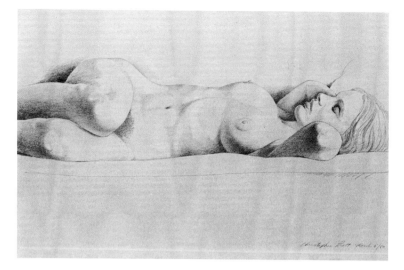

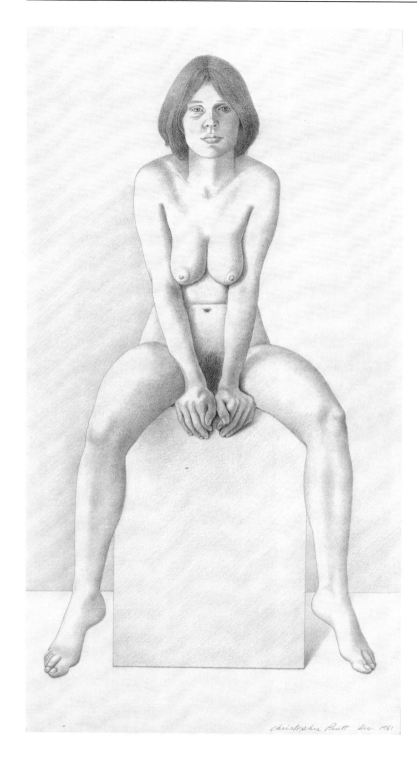

Girl Sitting on a box
1981
Graphite on paper
18″ x 10″
Private Collection

Girl Lying Down
1980
Graphite on paper
8½″ x 14″
Collection Mr. and Mrs.
Bill Campbell

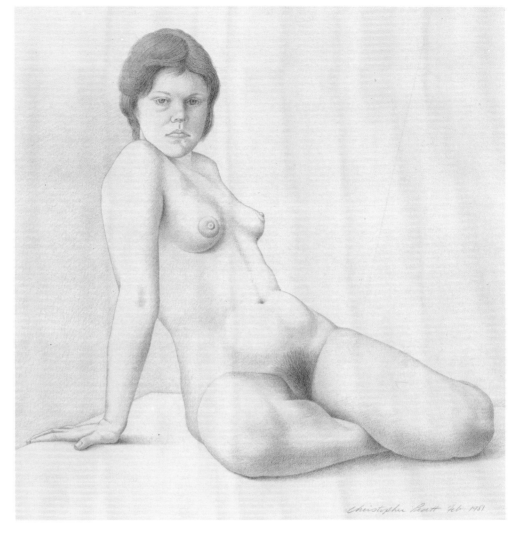

Marion
1980
Graphite on paper
10″ x 11″
Private Collection

Young Model
1981
Graphite on paper
10½″ x 10½″
Collection Mira Godard Gallery

This is an out-of-time, out-of-season image: no movement, nobody on deck to watch the sea go by, and distant drift ice on the horizon (that gave me another horizontal line to play with). My recollection is of some level crossing on a ferry between Nova Scotia and Newfoundland, just the throb of the engines and that straight, relentless push through the sea.

March Crossing — Deck Lines
1977
Original signed screenprint,
edition of 5
19½″ x 31½″

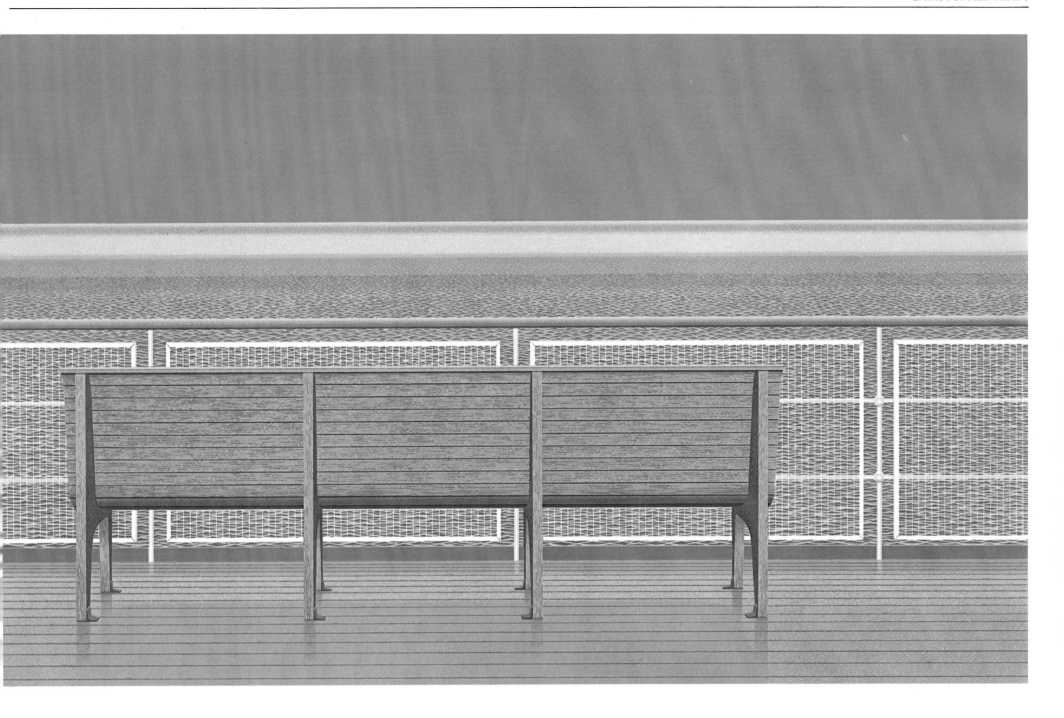

March Crossing
1977
Original signed screenprint,
edition of 48
19½″ x 31½″

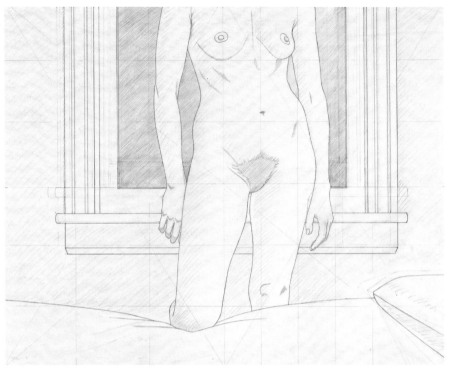

I had never done a lithograph before, but I always felt that the medium lent itself to night, to darkness, because of the rich inky blacks. Also, I had not used a figure in a print. So those things came together here. The medium influenced my approach to the figure. I provisionally titled the print 'Summer Place II'. The title 'Fisher's Maid' has nothing to do with anyone of that name.

Nude by Night Window
(Study for Fisher's Maid)
1977
Graphite on paper
5⅛″ x 5⅝″
Collection Mira Godard Gallery

Study for Fisher's Maid
1977
Graphite on paper
12″ x 15″
Collection the Artist

Fisher's Maid
1978
Original signed lithograph,
edition of 50
11¾″ x 15″

Basement Flat
1978
Oil on board
42″ x 42″
Lavalin Inc. Collection, Canada

Railway
1978
Original signed screenprint,
edition of 39
26″ x 30″

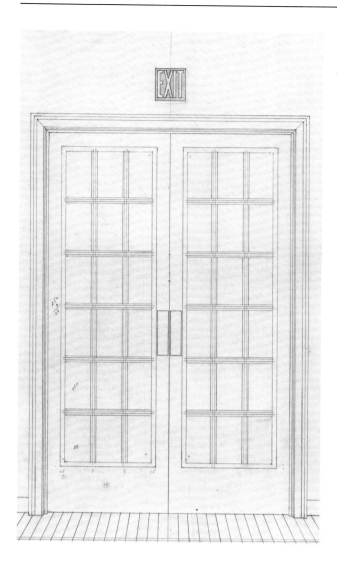

Some twelve years ago, walking down the corridor of an old hotel, I saw an exit sign and a pair of glass doors which reminded me of something. When I started playing with the idea, it turned into the gymnasium at Holloway, my public school, a dark, forbidding building backed up against a cliff. The green relates to the underground mood of the gymnasium and, for some reason, to the cold sound of running water.

Study for Exit
1978
Graphite on paper
14½″ x 8″
Collection the Artist

Exit
1978/79
Oil on board
51⅞″ x 32″
Polysar Collection

157

Above Montreal
1979
Original signed screenprint,
edition of 40
20″ x 23″

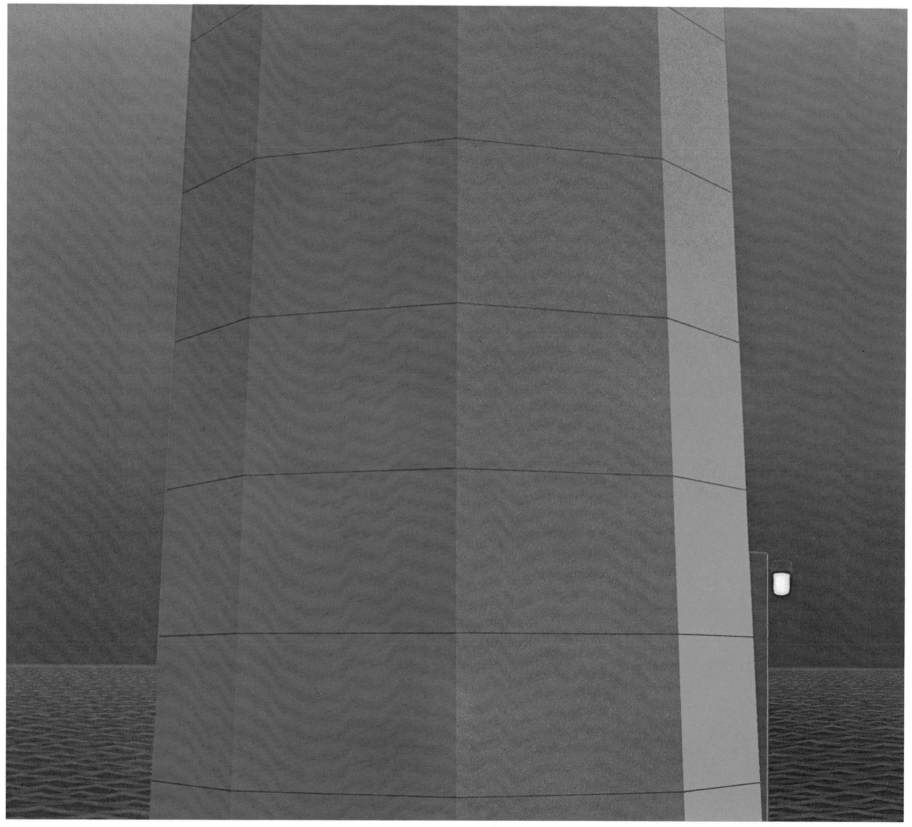

Light Northeast
1979
Original signed screenprint,
edition of 45
15″ x 17⅛″

159

My images are restorations of a kind. Like art, restorations always go beyond reality. They are abstractions, voids; walls without attackers; forts not under siege; old rooms without draughts; like this white lighthouse with no keeper, this wall facing west, with crisp, blue shadows cast by straight, fair boards and white walls glazed subtle blue and rose by the horizontal winter sun. 'Wall Facing West' and 'March Night' are the same subject done at different times in my life, and it's a subject I've thought a lot about and don't think is exhausted yet. I still think of doing it with tree shadows on the wall.

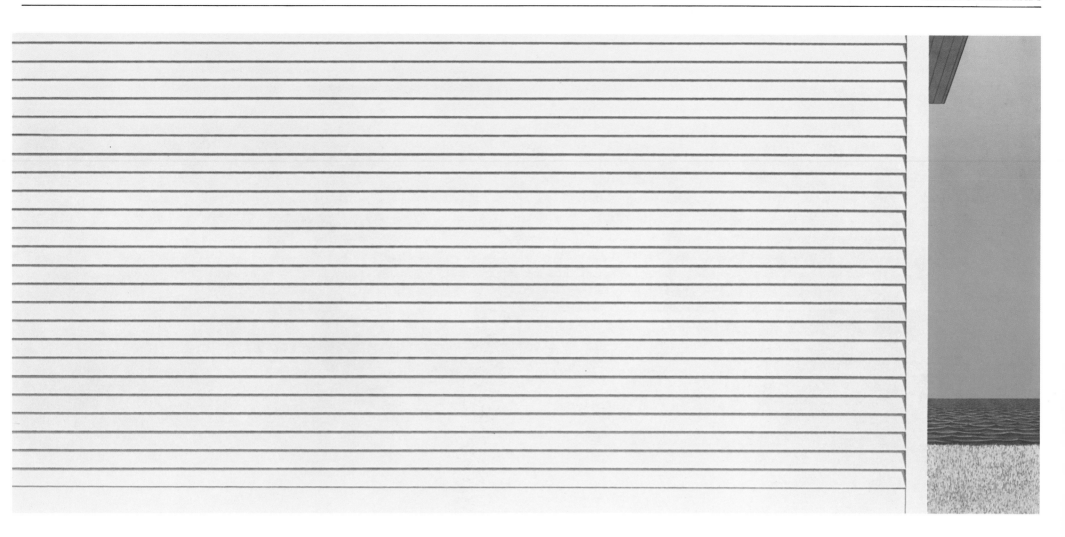

Wall Facing West
1980
Original signed screenprint,
edition of 50
14⅜" x 32"

Waves (Study for Labrador Sea)
1979
Graphite and wash on paper
8″ x 10″
Collection the Artist

Fog Bank (Study for
Western Shore)
1979
Coloured pencil on paper
8″ x 10″
Collection the Artist

Fog and Cliffs (Study for
Hawke Bay)
1980
Coloured pencil on paper
8″ x 10″
Collection the Artist

Western Shore
1979
Original signed screenprint,
edition of 93
8″ x 10″

Labrador Sea
1980
Original signed screenprint,
edition of 93
8″ x 10″

Hawke Bay
1980
Original signed screenprint,
edition of 93
8″ x 10″

165

166

Trunk
1979/80
Oil on board
36½″ x 42″
Private Collection

Bed and Blind
1980/81
Oil on board
26½" x 42"
Collection Secao Alcan Ltée

Dresser and Dark Window
1981
Oil on board
36½″ x 42″
Private Collection

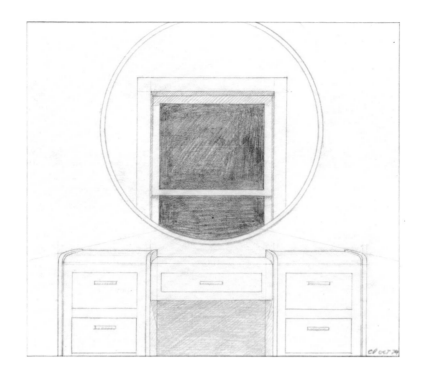

Study for Dresser and
Dark Window
1980
Graphite on paper
4¼″ x 5″
Collection the Artist

Study for Trunk
1979
Graphite on paper
4¼″ x 5″
Collection the Artist

I made the Stamp prints as a kind of souvenir of Newfoundland: not of Newfoundland as a place in the geographical sense, but as a concept — social, political, economic — that has passed. These early postage stamps seemed to me to constitute evidence of that Newfoundland.

The subjects are all actual Newfoundland postage stamps, dating from 1865 to 1887. In my prints they are enlarged by about twenty times. They are not, however, 'photographic' enlargements — the images I printed are not at all the same in texture or detail as they would be if they were direct photographic blow-ups. In making the stencils for the prints, I tried, in a way, to put myself in the roll of the original engraver: using the actual stamps as a model, I then proceeded to make the stencil as finely as I could. Therefore, for example, the lettering, and the curves in the decorative frills around the pictorial subject matter, are much crisper and more controlled than they would be in a photographic enlargement of the original engraving — such enlargement would, of course, magnify the difficulties encountered by even the most skilled engraver, working in such a minute scale as a postage stamp.

From a technical point of view, making these prints was something of a 'busman's holiday' for me. I rarely use lettering in my work, and never decorative scroll work, but I enjoy doing both — and making the stamp prints gave me a chance to do these things while working my hand around what was originally someone-else's image. Secondly, the prints relate to stamp collecting, which has interested me off and on since I was a boy.

Stamps have always appealed to me from a souvenir point of view, and, I suppose, as miniature works of art. I have always been attracted to individual stamps, or groups of stamps, more by their appearance than by their rarity or importance from a philatelist's point of view. But the serious philatelist's preoccupation with minor variations, or differences, in stamps that to the casual eye seemed to be the same — with subtle colour differences or slight variations in the engraving or perforation, interests me as well. In making these stamp prints, which I call the 'philatelic series', I also tried a play on that philatelic 'thing'. In each case, having made the basic stencil, I then used that stencil to do a variety of things; I tried slightly different colours and proved different papers, as presumably the original engraver would have done; I made some blocks; some of the stamps were done with perforations and without perforations. One thing I thought of doing, but never did, was to cancel some of the stamps with replicas of old, historically significant, post office marks. They would have related to the philatelic practice of collecting stamps 'on piece'. I did make up a stencil of such a cancellation, but in the end it seemed to trade on the nostalgia trip more than I wanted to — and in any case I couldn't bring myself to 'deface' the stamps I had made.

Victoria Regina
1971
Original signed screenprint,
edition of 36
30½″ x 22½″

Prince Albert
1974
Original signed screenprint,
edition of 36
30¾″ x 23¼″

1887 10¢ Black
1969
Original signed screenprint,
edition of 12
25⅝″ x 30″

The Stamp
1968
Original signed screenprint,
edition of 30
19½″ x 26½″

REFLECTIONS

Conversations with Christopher Pratt

Meriké Weiler

AN ART OBJECT MUST STAND ALONE, transcending its creator. And yet, at some moment, most of us have felt the urge to hear the voice and see the human hands behind the paint or stone or celluloid. That is what I felt the first time I saw the painting *Cottage* (frontispiece), with its intense, hypnotic calm, its geometric sea and sky, dusted with luminosity. I wanted to know more about the man who had painted such a passionately ordered universe.

It was in 1974 that I actually met Christopher Pratt, and since that time we have come to know each other well. Recently, I spent several days at the rambling, clapboard house in St. Mary's Bay, which has been his home for some twenty years. We talked about his life and work, and we travelled the barrens and the sea-washed cliffs of Newfoundland. Two impressions remain in my mind as the essence of those days of exploration.

One is the magic of hearing Pratt speak. Whether reminiscing or postulating or philosophizing, there is always a power to his thoughts. And though he is sometimes reluctant to reveal himself, there is always a poetry to his words.

The second impression that I bring from those days is broader, more difficult to describe. It is the sense that St. Mary's Bay, and beyond that, Newfoundland itself, is Pratt, that he has made himself in the image of the land, while at the same time allowing the elemental landscape to exert its power over him, moulding his character and creativity. To know Pratt is to know the land; and indeed, the converse is equally true.

I can think of no better way to describe the man than to give you the best of these two impressions: the words and the land.

Much of our time was spent in Pratt's studio. The room is sparse and white. In one corner, a Franklin stove stands on stubby legs. Beside it is an old, cream-coloured washbowl, brimming with smooth stones and shells, the souvenirs of hill and seaside walks, of islands visited by boat. Otherwise, the room is as efficient as the rigging of a sailing ship: grey, carpeted floor; grey drafting stool; a nondescript, brown couch; a wooden trunk for tools; a square, canvas-covered box, which alternates as table, chair, and stage; a metal drying-rack for silkscreen prints, and, in a low bookshelf, the only touch of luxury, a stereo. The room is softened by the light of the outdoors, light filtered by a large, black spruce just beyond the four-panelled window in the eastern wall. The window frames the flats and tidal pond of the Salmonier River, frozen and veiled in a wintery mist, and a range of low, wooded hills. Beyond stretch miles of wilderness, where ravens soar and herds of caribou roam free across the tundra uplands.

'Spiritually, I am so attached to my environment,' Pratt said, 'that if I ever had to leave Newfoundland, this house, I feel I could somehow return, walk up the river on the other side and, looking over, find myself still here, standing at this window. That feeling fascinates me and frightens me. Some people say my work is devoid of humanity, but I am in all my paintings, seeing if unseen. I am there to witness and recall. We think the dead are the ghosts, but the living also haunt.'

Is each work a recollection of a place he felt compelled to haunt?

'I never paint specifics. I shouldn't say "never." Sometimes I come close, and when I do, I think it's the weakest part of my work. But everything I do is informed and influenced by a range of experiences, encounters, and acquaintances. It's a collective, a generality. So there's ambiguity. I sometimes make an effort not to represent a particular time of day or a particular season. Because if a painting has no time, it has all time. Nearly everything I do is a mental or spiritual collage. Not in the sense that I take a wall from here and a window from there, but a collage conjured up from reactions and experiences that go back a long way, sometimes to childhood.'

Pratt uses his surroundings, the sea and barrens and open sky of Newfoundland, to make his art. He was born in St. John's on 9 December 1935. The older of two boys (his brother Philip, an architect, is ten years his junior), he grew up in St. John's like his father and grand-father before him. He is solidly part of the island's establishment.

'Actually, the two sides of my family are entirely different people.' His mother's family, the Dawes from Bay Roberts, was one of the original settling families, arriving in the 1700s, if not before. They were sea captains, merchants, entrepreneurs. Among other things, his seven uncles were in the fish trade and the lumber business. They ran a cooperage that made butter tubs and herring barrels; they sold coal and salt; they manufactured bricks and concrete blocks, built houses, and ran a tinsmith shop.

'I think it's the Dawe side of my nature to be emotional, the side that deals with content. And I think the formal aspect of my work—the discipline and conservatism, the tension and concern over having something right and not letting it go naked into the world—that originated in the Pratt side of my nature. There we trace back to a Methodist minister, Reverend John Pratt, who came to Newfoundland from Yorkshire in the mid-1800s and married a Newfoundland girl, named Fanny Knight.'

Though he was only three years old when the war broke out, Pratt remembers the North Atlantic convoys, the reality coloured and intensified by stories about the merchant fleets of Newfoundland, which once traded on the world market. He also remembers the oppressive basement flat of a three-story house on Le Marchant

Road. His family lived there until he was seven. Two of his Dawe uncles, who owned the house, occupied the upper floors.

'I have two very strong impressions from my childhood,' said Pratt. 'One has to do with ships, the other with rooms—the feeling of my bedroom, the ambience of the places where I visited or lived. The back of the flat on Le Marchant had a clear view of the St. John's harbour, but the front part was underground, funereal. I've had a fascination with and a horror of that kind of environment ever since.'

He paused, as if wondering if the significance of the memory was clear, then elaborated. 'I am genuinely moved by buildings, by shelters and windows and rooms made by man. That interest in architecture predates the composition and design: I sense a relationship between the house and the land and the sea and the people who were there or are there. But the geometry of architecture also appeals to me because it lends itself easily to the two-dimensional design techniques I use.'

Perhaps just as influential in later years as the architectural notions which were born in the basement flat were Pratt's early experiences with nature. 'When I was young,' he explained, 'my father worked long days—the Pratt family business was in wholesale hardware. But once or twice a summer he would come home early from the office (by that, I mean five o'clock), perhaps armed with an envelope of new trout flies, and we would drive out to Fourth Pond, five or six miles south of St. John's, and rent a boat to fish for trout.

'Those were very special evenings that I will always

own: the patterns of the flies we used (Black Gnat, Zulu, Paramachene Belle), the long June sunsets, and the songs of white-throated sparrows and hermit thrushes. Afterwards, we would visit with "Hen" Chafe, who rented us the boat. We'd talk by his kitchen stove about the days of bigger trout and about whether other patterns (Silver Doctor, Jenny Lind) would do the trick, and in the pauses, hear snipe winnowing, a haunting sound that catches in your throat.'

Pratt talked on about childhood summers spent blueberry picking and flycasting for salmon at Placentia, and about the autumn he stayed with his Aunt Jean in Bay Roberts, while the Pratt and Dawe families were building neighbouring houses in St. John's on Waterford Bridge Road. He was in grade three at the time and, arriving late in class, was put in the only seat available—next to a girl. 'There I was,' Pratt said with a smile, 'age eight, caught between the pot-bellied stove and the village beauty.'

But he had to overcome the stigma of being an outsider who couldn't row dories or climb wharves as well as the local kids. 'And they taunted me,' he said, 'as kids will, because I talked differently. But I managed, because I picked up the accent quickly. To this day, I can do a Bay Roberts accent verbatim and be mistaken for the genuine article. Or as they would say—the genuine *bahticle*.'

The outports and open landscape conditioned and influenced his understanding. 'I got a feeling for proportions, even for the level to which the blinds are drawn,' Pratt said, 'and for the smells and colours. *Landing* (page 113), for example, would be inconceivable in pink or blue. It had to be that particular apple green with white, like

177

many kitchens around St. Mary's Bay are to this day.'

By Christmas 1942, the family was settled in the new house on Waterford Bridge Road in St. John's, and Pratt had returned to the local school, named Holloway.

'Art was beginning to give me an identity,' he said with hindsight. 'It was the counterbalance to the things I couldn't do. Thinking back, I can recognize things that made my becoming an artist inevitable—the papier-mâché head I made in grade three that went far beyond the bounds of the assignment. I was afraid I would be penalized for my "exuberance," but my teacher rewarded me with praise and recognition for my creativity—and my talent. And she often chose me to draw the diagrams or lesson illustrations on the blackboard. I know now that those moments were significant.'

It was a long jaunt to Holloway, a ponderous pile of red brick, backed up against a cliff. Pratt and his cousins sometimes took the streetcar home, but even that stopped half a mile from where they lived, so there was always a wintertime slog through the snow. The dark gymnasium, the theme of *Exit* (page 157), terrified him, with its small, high windows, almost smothered by the cliff, and an exercise device, a 'ladder,' suspended in a zigzag from the ceiling. For Pratt, that ladder symbolizes the dark side of childhood, the failures that only success in art could truly offset.

'I may well have been the only kid who never had the nerve to jump and shinny up that ladder. I felt emotionally trapped. I could see no exit. The feeling haunts me still, of not being up to the mark, not being able to compete.' So although he loved sports, such as softball and skating on the river, he came to dread school sports.

After finishing grade six at Holloway, Pratt went to the Prince of Wales College. As we talked about those years, he worried a loose thread on his shirt-sleeve, trying to define his character: half-introvert, half-extrovert. The same holds true today. Pratt can be formal, detached, circumspect. He also indulges in raffish and irreverent wit, raising the joke to a fine art form.

At school he did all the normal things boys do—performing, working on the yearbook, and, in his spare time, collecting the stamps of Newfoundland. And in his final year, he managed, just managed, to get on the hockey team, although he claims he was very much 'the fifteenth pair of skates.'

'Actually,' he said with a grin, 'I was a budding extrovert. I was always getting involved in some sort of shenanigan. When I was in grade ten (I think it was grade ten), our class was put in charge of the hot dogs for the annual Ladies' Aid Society. Being a rather avant-garde lot, we decided we were going to serve hamburgers instead. Now I won't get into telling you my part in this revolutionary act—that would be "telling tales out of school"—but silly as it now sounds, ten years later I was still remembered, in some circles, for the uproar it caused.

'I also had a lonely streak,' he continued, 'but it wasn't too apparent. And I was starting to get abstract in the way I thought.' He created his own private world, daydreaming of summertime and of trout fishing along the western shore of St. Mary's Bay.

By the time he was thirteen, Christopher Pratt had a strong sense of what he wanted to do. 'I can remember seeing one girl walking in Waterford Bridge Road with a handful of watercolour brushes, presumably coming from an art class, and having the distinct feeling that she hadn't any right to them, since painting was my legitimate trade.'

But St. John's, at least as Pratt knew it in the forties and fifties, was hardly fertile ground for the visual arts: no professional painters, no art on the walls, nothing to encourage a young artist. However, the fact that his grandfather Pratt, a businessman and a solid conservative, was a hobby watercolourist did give some legitimacy to the urge. 'Obviously I wouldn't consider painting a sissy thing if my grandfather did it.'

But in retrospect, there was more: a concrete need to paint. 'I wanted to record places I'd been and experiences I'd had: to keep a visual diary. It never occurred to me to use photography. And it never occurred to me that I could paint as a career. I mean, how the hell would you make a living?'

Pratt went to Memorial University in St. John's and enrolled in engineering. He passed half his courses and failed the other half. Pratt remembers the year as one of confusion—and as one in which the old contrast of 'success in papier-mâché versus failure on the exercise ladder' reasserted itself. He won first prize for water-colour in the Government of Newfoundland Arts and Let-ters Competition, but still, his future seemed uncertain.

'I was the ripe old age of seventeen and didn't know where I was going.' But the drafting he learned that year still plays a part in the way he lays out an image, and surveying techniques, such as triangulation, influence the design and physical balance of his work. Surveying also led to summer jobs at the American naval base in Argentia and that, in turn, led to the painting *Federal Area* (page 121) and to a love/hate relationship with institutions and their claustrophobic schedules and controls.

Later that year, 1953, he registered in the pre-med science programme at Mount Allison University in New Brunswick. 'My mother had been a nurse,' he said, 'and she was preoccupied with the possibility that I might discover a cure for some terrible thing. But the thought of confronting someone else's liver was more than I could bear. Still, I set off, taking along some of my watercolours, which I showed to the staff in the Fine Arts Department. On seeing what I had, Professor Lawren Harris, Jr., the head of the school, wrote to my father suggesting I take art, but Dad, although impressed, thought Harris "must have one loose"—who in his right mind would encourage a young man to take art?

'Anyway, I wasn't enthusiastic about medicine, so the next year I switched to general arts, majoring in English.' He discovered he wasn't enthusiastic about that either. Halfway through his third year, Pratt reached a decision. 'One afternoon in December, I just got fed up, and I went to see the president of Mount Allison University and said, melodramatically, "Dr. Flemington, I'm going to be a painter."'

With that sentence, he abandoned his efforts to become an engineer, a doctor, a journalist. He left without a degree but with the friendship of a bright, brunette art student named Mary West, and he went home to Newfoundland to paint full-time, turning out dozens of watercolours and selling every one.

'It was a breathing space,' Pratt says now of those two years back home, 'a way to ship out some of the wreckage, the failures. University was an alien, black and white

179

experience. But contrary to stories that I was eternally lonely and brooding, I'd like it on record that I was often down at the local honky-tonk, playing the piano, which I don't do very well, surrounded by ten or fifteen kids.'

At home there were different pressures. 'I felt the constraints of working in my bedroom, knowing nothing about any medium other than watercolour, with neighbours thinking I was "unemployed." So I knew I had to go to art school, in a way to legitimize this thing. And I had to struggle, often painting subjects to which I wasn't too committed anymore—picturesque landscapes, dories. It's the only period in my career when painting had that aspect of a job. It taught me what I didn't want to do. I've never accepted a commission since.'

Christopher Pratt and Mary West were married in Fredericton, New Brunswick on 12 September 1957. Two days later, in Halifax, they boarded a small oceanliner, bound for Scotland and the Glasgow School of Art.

As Pratt described his discovery of Mary at Mount Allison University, I felt that what he was alluding to was destiny, without wanting to use the word. 'Mary rescued me from my indecision, from my lack of self-esteem and worth. She is an extraordinary person: intelligent, compassionate, and incredibly moral. She has everything in the most exquisite balance possible. The world would be a better place if everyone could have a wife like Mary. . . . It may sound excessively romantic, but the minute I saw her, I had a premonition. I felt there was something there. Some of us are blessed, I think. Some of us walk in the right door at the right time.'

When Christopher and Mary were married, one of his relatives suggested that part of Mary's job was to keep his feet on the ground. 'Oh no,' replied Mary, 'my job is to keep his head in the clouds.' She has more than kept her word over the years.

The Glasgow years deepened Pratt's commitment to his work. The largely academic training suited him. He studied design, perspective, anatomy, life drawing, graphics—all the basics. He found the new environment both exciting and unsettling. For two years he spent close to ten hours every day honing his technique.

'I had a wonderful teacher, an old-line academic—again a *she*, like most of the influential people in my life. At least once a day she would say, "Art is not reality." Even though we had to draw as if we were making maps, she kept insisting, "Art is not reality." I still proceed from that premise. Sometimes the encounter with an object is catalytic: you recognize a set of relationships which has just been subconscious before. But the art object has to stand on its own feet, independent of the real object which precipitated it.

'The way I approach realism, my concern with design and form, I either learned myself or learned in Glasgow, though it's fair to say my preoccupations were enforced rather than initiated there. We drew incessantly from plaster casts. I still draw the figure the way I learned to draw a plaster cast—in terms of its volumes, as opposed to its irregularities. I'm more concerned with giving a thing shape, making a leg look round if it's round, square if it's square, than I am with copying wrinkles or moles or the way light falls accidentally.'

In addition to the regular studio work, students were required to do a painting on an assigned subject each month and to present the work in class for critiques by visiting professors. There were no holds barred. 'I remember one professor saying (not to me), "I could knit a better picture." But teacher after teacher used to say about my work, "It's very North American." That pleased me greatly because I always attached a particular value to doing my own thing. I believed that "honest" art would automatically reflect its own occasion, its own environment, even if it did not identify that environment in terms of subject matter.'

Many of his fellow students were concerned with the latest thing in Paris and painted in a *Tachiste* style. They praised each other with, 'Ach, that's very *tache*.' For Pratt, that was the wrong approach. At a time when North American artists could be divided into those who had their crisis when they got to Europe and those who had it when they got back, Pratt never had a crisis. And never got to Paris.

'I've still never been,' he said. Why didn't he go when he and Mary were in Glasgow? 'My father was helping us and Mary's, too. We didn't want to indulge ourselves on anybody's handout.' He hastened to add, however, that lack of emotional need was as significant as lack of money. 'I've never felt the necessity to travel. Mind you, I've been to New York. Twice. Once in 1955, for a week. And once for a day. That was in 1976, when I had an exhibition at the Marlborough Gallery. I found spending just a few hours in the Museum of Modern Art was an extraordinary, exhilarating experience. I'm not sure that spending a month there would be much better. A walk through is enough to put everything in perspective, to tell you where you stand in the great scheme of things, to give you bench marks.

'A small Paul Klee really impressed me and a Modigliani nude. I'm not a fan of his, but the richness of the paint and the handling of the figure was such an antithesis to my poverty-stricken approach. . . . But what overwhelmed me was the sense of quality. It reassured me that the visual arts have substance, that they are "for real," in social terms, like engineering, music, catching fish; it confirmed my role, confirmed that I was engaged in a legitimate pursuit, not something doomed to be irrelevant in the real world. That was the important part of that visit.'

I asked whether the years in Glasgow appreciably altered his style and technique. 'Yes and no,' he said. 'I tended to protect and nourish what I had brought with me. I was conservative, although coming from North America you were expected to be avant-garde, and that tended to isolate me and, ironically, got my work off in a conservative vein. I went there with an open mind. But, the very first day in drawing class, I was drawing apples fairly freely when the teacher came along. "More precision, more precision," she said. So I sharpened my pencil and gave her an apple that looked as if it had been drawn with a steel wire.'

Glasgow proved catalytic. In his two-year stay, Pratt came to clearly recognize his subject matter: architecture and light. His first act was to accept it; later, he transformed matter into mystery.

It was just ten years after the war. Glasgow was subdued and dark, heavy with coal smoke. 'Day after day, all you could see was this pale orange ball through the pervasive grey. Atmospherically, it appealed to me, the varieties of grey and black. I was overwhelmed there by right angles: tenements built of great rectangular blocks of stone, acres of façades with infinitely varied windows, like little abstracts.

'We were given "a view from a window" as an assignment my first term. Mary and I were holed up in a tiny flat, so I did a watercolour of the lane behind us, verbatim, inventing a figure (we always had to put a figure in) trudging home with his copy of *The Scotsman*. For me, it was an opportunity to strut my stuff.' He pulled out everything he had taught himself about perspective, tonal recession, and reflections. The result was *Grosvenor Crescent* (page 41). The watercolour caught the eye of the director, who displayed it conspicuously in the school gallery.

'That was a taste of honey. Remember, one of the reasons I went into art, as opposed to engineering, was because of an early taste of honey—maybe not the big leagues, but for three years running, I'd won the watercolour prize in the Government of Newfoundland Arts and Letters Competition. And at Mount Allison, though I wasn't in fine arts, I was appointed decorations chairman for the junior prom. Like everybody else, I wanted an identity. I wanted to be known for something other than my social insurance number. Art was something that I did well, that I enjoyed. Art gave me an identity.'

What were the striking features of the Glasgow years? The question brought us to the leitmotifs of Pratt's personality: conservatism and control.

'I have a horror of disorder,' he said, 'of things that are outside my control or, in effect, outside the control of humankind. One of the things I liked about Scotland was the fact that the imprint of man was virtually everywhere.

What seemed at a superficial glance to be wild country, was in fact areas walled off with rock. And forests often were planted and rectangular. (This is in striking contrast to Newfoundland, which is overwhelmingly wild country.) I like the regularity of fences, the security of rectangles imposed on the land, because that shows man in control. I find that comforting. My architectural straight lines relate to organization and control and the presence of man— even my landscapes have long horizons, the ultimate straight line in nature.'

He paused to consider. 'In some ways, I am or try to be, a temperate, conservative person. At least I always play it safe. I have never set off on an adventure without careful preparation. Although I'm often troubled with spectres of greener grass, I've lived in the same house, in the same valley, by the same river, and done virtually the same thing, every day for nearly twenty years. I have a puritanical notion that things ought to be ordinary, not ostentatious. I believe things are better when they're not in excess, when they're measured and held in check.

'In reality, I'm quite an emotional person. I am easily moved to tears. And so why do I work the way I do? Why do I refuse to put all kinds of lovely bits of business in my paintings? I think it has to do with this: there was such a destructive lack of self-control in people close to me when I was young that I determined consciously to stay on track. My paintings are my rails.'

The decision to leave Glasgow and return to Canada was a facet of the determination to 'stay on track.' 'It was my need to play it safe again. Technically, I probably suffered from the decision. But we had very little money, we had a child (John was born in July 1958), and we both wanted to live in Atlantic Canada. Too, it was a return to home, to roots. My spirit of adventure wasn't strong.'

The question was, how to make a living? 'The only thing I could think of was teaching, but jobs were few and far between. In reality, the main reason I wound up back at Mount Allison in 1959 was so I'd be on-site in the Maritimes if anything came up.'

Christopher and Mary rented a small house in Sackville from the university, and Christopher set up his studio there. He lugged home a silkscreen frame and started making prints, periodically taking his completed work back to school for grades and critiques. His teachers, Alex Colville, Lawren Harris, Jr., and Ted Pulford, encouraged him, bent the regulations a bit, and treated him more or less as a professional on campus, although he and Mary were both enrolled as students.

His print *Boat in Sand* (page 47), a daydream of a trap skiff washed up on a Newfoundland shore, sold briskly to his fellow students and was purchased by the National Gallery of Canada during its Fourth Biennial Exhibition of Canadian Art in 1961. Another print, *Haystacks in December* (page 43), was exhibited the same year in the Young Contemporaries show in London, Ontario. And his painting *Demolitions on the South Side* (page 45) won second prize at the Atlantic Awards Exhibition of Dalhousie University in Halifax. 'I got my foot in the door professionally while I was still a student,' Pratt said.

In 1961, both Christopher and Mary graduated from Mount Allison with Bachelor of Fine Arts degrees. By then, Christopher was well on his way with awards, sales, and some degree of fame. There was also a job offer back home in Newfoundland. His plan had worked better (or perhaps worse) than he'd intended. The job, which involved running the art gallery for Memorial University and teaching painting at night, soon became a terrible frustration.

'I had to go to a certain place, at a certain time, and sit behind a certain desk, whether I wanted to or not. That wasn't my idea of regularity! I loathed the whole thing. I asked one woman why she came to class. Because her husband went curling Thursday nights, she said. Those were probably the two and a half most wretched years of my life. My father used to say, "You studied art, you're supposed to be an artist, doing paintings. What are you doing there, working for a mediocre salary?"'

Finally, between his father's advice, his doctor's advice, and his own instinct for survival, he quit, on the verge of a nervous breakdown. So one spring day, when he was twenty-eight years old, he piled Mary and the three kids in a car (Anne was born in 1960, Barbara in 1963), quit the security of a steady job, quit St. John's, and headed for an old summer place his father had bought in St. Mary's Bay. 'I thought, well, we'll live here for a year and get our feet on the ground. . . . That was a long time ago. In one sense, I date myself as an artist from that Christmas in 1955 when I quit Mount Allison. And in another, from the spring of 1963, when I moved to St. Mary's Bay.'

When he was young, cooped up in the city, Pratt often dreamed of the open sea, of rivers full of silver trout, and of flights of ducks, patterned across the sky. 'About three days after we moved here,' he said, 'I woke up suddenly at dawn and went to the window. At first, I thought I was still dreaming. There was low sunlight and a mist along the river and a flock of eider ducks, black and white with pale green headdresses, flying up the river through the fog. It was magic, and I took it as a sign.

'I still like it here,' Pratt went on to say. 'I wake up in the morning and I'm happy to be here. I like to work intimately with my environment. I go to the same places year after year—the hill across the river, for example—and each time it's a new experience. I still believe that less is more.'

The years since the move to St. Mary's Bay blend together in Pratt's mind. His youngest son, Ned, was born there in 1964. The four children have grown up beside the river. In the winters, they skated on their frozen river-pond. On Indian summer mornings, they swam and sailed and fished there, reeling in salmon and trout at the bottom of the grassy garden, as sunrise glinted through the valley haze. Gulls, geese, and ospreys would skim overhead, and sometimes seals and otters would lollop in the river and moose would wander down from the dark woods to stand in the shallows at the other side.

'I think the one time in my career I tried to anticipate what people would say about my work was around 1964,' Pratt said, 'when there was a spate of nationalism, a great Canadian talent hunt. I was terrified that I would be included in the mainland shows on a geographical, rather than a quality, basis. You know, "Let's get the tenth province in." I don't believe in that. So rather than a cove or fish-flake or the usual romantic, seaside bric-a-brac, I wanted to use subject matter not particular to Newfoundland. And since I genuinely wanted to do female figures, I began to paint them, starting with *Woman at a Dresser* (page 61), which was my first figure and which became the first in a number of bedroom paintings.

'I feel professionally shortchanged when I can't paint figures,' he continued, 'but I never paint males. I have zero interest in the male figure. In fact, I'd be very embarrassed in the presence of a male model. One could psychoanalyse and maybe come up with answers, but I just don't get along as well with men. Most of my professional dealings are with women.' Pratt reflected for several minutes, then continued. 'There are always two figures in my figure paintings—the girl and me. I have tried many times to paint a second figure, but I've always eliminated it, because three is a crowd, and I can be an intensely jealous person.

'I have to be alone, completely by myself, before I can start work. I often work on figures after the model has left the room, so that the work can liberate itself from her—she is herself, *this* is mine. In some cases, I've put a woman in and painted her out again to be alone—in *Subdivision* and *Night Window* (pages 114, 11), for example. Also, because I didn't want to tell a story. I mean, I don't have a set of rules that says: Thou shalt not paint pictures that tell stories, but I instinctively back away.'

Pratt has a fascination for places out-of-season: for rivers when the salmon run is past, for cottages in spring or winter, 'when it's cold and musty and secretive. It may relate to my desire to possess. There is no competition; I have privacy. It is strange territory then, with hidden tensions, and comes close, in some dimensions, to a sexual experience. . . . I consider painting to be a private act, but it's not a look through a keyhole. I want the woman to be unconcerned, not unaware. The viewer is welcome. But I am the viewer. I don't care about any other viewer. I am making an object for myself, and I am concerned that there is no rejection of me. I like to feel that people who pose for me want to be there, that they consider it a privilege, arrogant as that may sound.'

Getting models has been a continuing problem, since the only sources are the small neighbouring communities of Mt. Carmel and St. Catherine's. Why not use Mary, then, as a model, the way Edward Hopper (an artist whose work influenced Pratt) used his wife?

'From time to time, I joke,' said Pratt, 'that I don't draw my wife because it's not as much fun. But the reasons are more complex. Mary has her own work to do. Second, just as I wouldn't draw the same house all the time (although I've been accused of that), I wouldn't want to draw the same person all the time. Also, working at home, I don't have much professional privacy. When my children were young—God knows what effect it had on them—they may have wondered why Daddy was locked up in his studio with a girl who had no clothes on. People used to ask, "Don't you think the kids feel funny about that?" But I always thought they would feel funnier if their mother was locked up with me, because they cared for her, and then they'd see the drawing, which I felt might trouble them. They didn't care about the others. I've never hidden any of my work from my children.'

So how does he solve the problem of finding models? The approach over the years has been piecemeal, a matter of change and the moment. 'Usually what happens is that someone who comes to work in the kitchen, by a slow process, a long protracted series of mini-unveilings, winds up posing for me. As Mary says, "Familiarity breeds consent."'

Most of the early figures are shown from the back because Pratt wanted them anonymous, and because the forms in the back are simpler. 'Occasionally I've come close to being specific,' he said. 'The figure in *Apartment* (page 125) is close to being a specific girl, though not the one who posed for it. The most specific figure is in *French Door* (page 112). She lived with us for three years, did the housework, posed for me.

'I always felt that she was just on the periphery, endangered, exposed to our ideas, which were not viable for her. She was outside, looking in. She wasn't part of our lives. . . . But we were dominating hers—I saw that after she had left. I did the painting then.

'For me, painting nudes is a busman's holiday. It's fun; it reassures me. I don't work at making them polite. Still, although people see phallic intent in the bedpost sticking up in the painting *Young Woman Dressing* (page 63), I have been accused of creating the most lifeless, bloodless, sexless nudes in the history of art.'

On the last day of my stay, Pratt and I decided to take a drive along the craggy coast. The silver station wagon headed south along the eastern shore of St. Mary's Bay, through Forest Field, St. Joseph's, and Riverhead, through Path End and the Gaskiers, where the cold grey sea slices and sculpts the barren rock into low cliffs, bays, and headlands, just as it has done for centuries.

Our conversation that day seemed as unpredictable as the land, lurching from reflections to work, to the past, to philosophy. At one point we walked along the shore, and

Pratt wove memories, casting a verbal image of himself, the artist reflected in nature.

'You know, salmon lie where the current is most comfortable. One year there was a tiny grilse in our river, with an x-shaped mark (perhaps a seal bit it). Whenever the tide turned and the current changed, it would move. But it always returned to the same spot. I think I'm instinctively seeking out or making a more comfortable, secure place in the same way. That means painting to address anxiety—to escape. I started out painting as an escape, to re-create, to isolate, the quality of being over at Little Barrisway or Little Salmonier; eternally fishing for trout on a July morning was far more pleasant than studying at university or living in St. John's, and I wanted to preserve that.'

But Pratt's paintings could never be called mementos. To make them so would contravene his own artistic vision. 'If I have a key philosophy, it's that art objects should be complete in themselves, without reference to anything or anyone else. They should exist as if born with their identity. I am fascinated by the hours of darkness. I mean physical darkness, but you can't use the word without running into philosophical overtones—"heart of darkness." For example, I've just finished a working drawing, an hours-of-darkness image. It's the essence of my childhood recollections of Christmas: a cardboard wreath wrapped in raffia, with an electric candle, hanging in the window. We had wreaths like that in the basement flat. I call it *Last Christmas*. Obviously a word like "end" or "last" allows for all kinds of interpretations. This one represents the last Christmas of a certain kind. It happened when I was seven, about the time we moved out. . . . Before, I had one feeling about Christmas and Santa Claus, and afterwards, an entirely different one.

Maybe it's the end of innocence.

'It's an extraordinarily austere image: a circle in a square floating against a distant grey sky, and at the bottom, a barren expanse of snow. Or maybe, frozen sea. An austere image, and yet, it says Christmas to me.'

The sea-lined road sloped down from Gaskiers, curved to the left and then charged straight across the black sand of St. Vincent's Beach. Beyond, was the inlet of Peter's River. Pratt stopped the car and we both reflected on the scene for several minutes. It was he who broke the silence.

'My paintings are remains, the remains of a mental process. They are abandoned; they are never finished. Because you don't really come to the end of any thought process, but you sure as hell come to the end of a capacity to focus. I have never been completely satisfied with a painting. The realization, the representation of an idea, dangles in front of you like a carrot. You never quite get it. When I finish a painting, I can't stand to look at it anymore. I'm disappointed, frequently despondent. And exhausted. I have great crises, doubts. Once upon a time I used to throw things in the garbage can.'

We drove east into the immense, lunar landscape of the St. Shott's Barrens. There were gullies and rills filled with snow and groves of stunted spruce and larch with wind-shaved tops. Dark mosses and ochre patches of sedge and cotton grass shaded hollows and hillocks. Scrub clusters of blueberry and Labrador tea filled the spaces between huge boulders, once left as glacial debris. And there were wild rose bushes with burnt sienna leaves and the dark, acid, purple-greys of alder bushes.

We left the barrens behind. Soon there were stake and rail fences again, patchworking the land, flocks of sheep in the rock-strewn pastures, and wooden houses, four-square and functional, huddled helter-skelter along the road and spilling down to the sea.

There was a feeling of freedom as the car rolled over the crest of a hill and an immense vista opened out: a rise of barren land—Cape Spear, the furthest point east in North America—angling over the Atlantic and the open sky. Pratt stopped the car again. We climbed the steep rock up to a deserted lighthouse and an empty clapboard house, solitary forms sluiced to a shine by seawind and light.

'I can look over the Atlantic,' Pratt said, 'and see as much space as I can see from anywhere on earth, presumably. And I can look over vast stretches of barren land where nobody lives. I can see huge geographies. This has left me with a sense of openness. . . .

'Remember, I grew up with stories about ships and schooners, destroyers in the war. For me, as a boy,' Pratt said, 'the measure of a man was his capacity to take a ship to sea. I became an artist by a strange process. If I had had the courage or strength, I would have liked to become a sea captain.'

What, in the end, was that strange process, I asked. Whence the artist? The answer, like the man, was philosophical. 'I can remember—I couldn't have been more than four or five—getting into a cold sweat, shivering with the realization that things exist and the absurdity of that. Although it's equally impossible to conceive of total nothingness. There must be other life somewhere. There must be other balls of chemicals and energies like ours. And yet, we face the possibility that we are at the apex of all things, the highest manifestation of the basic stuff that emanates from the fact that there is anything at all.

'Now, if this basic stuff is energy, and energy becomes matter, and matter becomes animal, and animal becomes self-aware, and self-aware becomes self-controlling—we're faced with the possibility that we are a stage in the evolution of God. Because if we can learn enough about the elemental stuff to influence its ongoing . . .

'I think that the creative act—what painters and poets do and engineers and scientists—is at the forefront of human experience, the apex, the apogee of this basic stuff. Because, however pretentious it may sound, to be creative is to be God-like. You are at the heat shield of this thrust of energy, en route to the evolution of God.'

EXHIBITIONS

1961-1968
Successive Biennials at the National Gallery of Canada,
Ottawa, Ontario

1961
9th Annual Young Contemporaries Exhibition, London Public
Library and Art Museum, London, Ontario
Atlantic Awards Exhibition, Dalhousie Art Gallery,
Dalhousie University, Halifax, Nova Scotia
Canadian Society of Graphic Arts

1962
First Biennial Winnipeg Show, Winnipeg Art Gallery,
Winnipeg, Manitoba

1963
Winnipeg Exposition, Winnipeg Art Gallery, Winnipeg, Manitoba

1965
Solo Exhibition, Memorial University Art Gallery, St. John's,
Newfoundland
Atlantic Provinces Art Circuit: Memorial University Art Gallery;
Dalhousie Art Gallery; Owens Art Gallery, Mount Allison University;
Confederation Centre Art Gallery and Museum; University of New
Brunswick Art Centre

1966
Magic Realism, London Public Library and Art Museum,
London, Ontario
Canadian Society of Graphic Arts (successive exhibitions)
Artists of Atlantic Canada, Memorial University Art Gallery,
St. John's, Newfoundland

1967
Second Atlantic Awards Exhibition, Dalhousie Art Gallery,
Dalhousie University, Halifax, Nova Scotia

1968
Kingston Spring Exhibition of Art, Agnes Etherington Art Centre,
Kingston, Ontario

1970
Vancouver Art Gallery, Vancouver, British Columbia (originated
from Memorial University Art Gallery, St. John's, Newfoundland)
Solo Exhibition, Godard Lefort Gallery, Vancouver, British Columbia

1971
Marlborough Godard Gallery, Montreal, Quebec

1972
Solo Exhibition, Memorial University Art Gallery, St. John's,
Newfoundland

1973
Canada Trajectoire, Musée d'Art Moderne, Paris, France
Christopher Pratt Serigraphs, Beaverbrook Art Gallery, Fredericton,
New Brunswick

1974
Marlborough Godard Gallery, Toronto, Ontario
Thirteen Artists from Marlborough Godard, Marlborough Galleries,
New York, New York

1975
The Canadian Canvas, Art Gallery of Ontario, Toronto, Ontario

1975-76
Wallace S. Bird Collection, Beaverbrook Art Gallery, Fredericton,
New Brunswick. Touring Mendel Art Gallery and Conservatory,
Saskatoon, Art Gallery of Nova Scotia, New Brunswick Museum,
Galerie Restigouche, Memorial University Art Gallery
Acute Image, Owens Art Gallery, Mount Allison University, Sackville,
New Brunswick

1976
Marlborough Galleries, New York, New York
Marlborough Godard Gallery, Montreal, Quebec and Toronto, Ontario
Twenty Canadians, Douglas Gallery, Vancouver, British Columbia

1976-78
Aspects of Realism, travelling exhibition organized by Rothmans of
Pall Mall Canada Limited

1977
Yves Gaucher and Christopher Pratt, Print Retrospectives, Vancouver
Art Gallery, Vancouver, British Columbia (in collaboration with
Mira Godard Gallery, Toronto)

1978
Mira Godard Gallery, Toronto, Ontario

1979-80
Aspects of Canadian Printmaking, travelling exhibition organized by
Mira Godard Gallery, Toronto, Ontario

1980
Solo Exhibition, Memorial University Art Gallery, St. John's,
Newfoundland
Mira Godard Gallery, Toronto, Ontario

1981
Correspondences, travelling exhibition organized by the Banff Centre
School of Fine Arts, Walter Phillips Gallery, Banff, Alberta

1982
Twenty-one: Drawings, Mira Godard Gallery, Toronto, Ontario

INDEX TO THE PLATES

CHRISTOPHER PRATT

Cottage
1973
Oil on board
26½" x 48"
Private Collection

The spirit and soul of all 33 million Canadians has been sewn into the fabric of these Winter Games.
This journey has not been about the few but rather the many.

L'esprit et l'âme des 33 millions de Canadiens ont imprégné le tissu de ces Jeux d'hiver.
Cette expérience a su toucher l'ensemble d'un peuple et on n'a mis personne de côté.

John Furlong

Editor / *Rédactrice* : Alison Gardiner **Design direction** / *Direction de la conception* : Leo Obstbaum **Design** / *Conception* : Teena Aujla, Chloé Douglas, Greg Durrell, Ben Hulse and/*et* Margaret Ko **Production design and management** / *Conception et gestion de la production* : Yumi White **Exclusive photography** / *Photographie exclusive* : Rick Collins, Ben Hulse, Blake Jorgenson, Sterling Lorence, David Martin and/*et* Steve Simon (see pg 397 for reference / *voir la page 397 pour référence*) **Colour correction** / *Correction des couleurs* : Vairdy Andrew and/*et* Ben Hulse **Photo and research assistance** / *Assistance à la photographie et à la recherche* : Roseanne Hinmueller

Feature writing / *Rédaction des articles vedettes* : Dianna Carr (Alpine Skiing / *Ski alpin*, Luge, Skeleton, Bobsleigh, Paralympic Alpine Skiing / *Ski alpin paralympique*) , Scott Colbourne (Cultural Olympiad / *Olympiade culturelle*), Chris Fair (Speed Skating / *Patinage de vitesse*, Curling, Wheelchair Curling / *Curling en fauteuil roulant*), Cindy Filipenko (Ski Jumping / *Saut à ski*, Nordic Combined / *Combiné nordique*, Cross-Country Skiing / *Ski de fond*, Biathlon, Paralympic Cross-Country Skiing / *Ski de fond paralympique*, Paralympic Biathlon / *Biathlon paralympique*), Alison Gardiner (Journey to 2010 / *Vers Vancouver 2010*, Media and Technology / *Médias et technologie*, Design / *Conception*, Ice Hockey introduction / *Introduction du hockey sur glace*), Beth Hornby (Figure Skating / *Patinage artistique*, Short Track Speed Skating / *Patinage de vitesse sur piste courte*), Lianne Kerr (Olympic Torch Relay / *Relais de la flamme olympique*, Freestyle Skiing / *Ski acrobatique*, Snowboard / *Surf des neiges*), Claudia Larouche (Paralympic Torch Relay / *Relais de la flamme paralympique*), David Martin (Olympic and Paralympic Opening and Closing Ceremonies / *Cérémonies d'ouverture et de clôture olympiques et paralympiques*, Olympic Village / *Village olympique*, Volunteers / *Bénévoles*, Spirit and Atmosphere / *Esprit et atmosphère*, The Canada that was, and the Canada that now is / *Le Canada d'hier, et le Canada d'aujourd'hui*), Don Wells (Ice Hockey / *Hockey sur glace*, Ice Sledge Hockey / *Hockey sur luge*)

Copyediting (English) / *Travail éditorial (anglais)* : Andrew Tzembelicos **Proofreading (English)** / *Lecture d'épreuves (anglais)* : Segun Afolabi **Fact-checking** / *Vérification des faits* : Holly Munn, Mark Woo and/*et* Vince Yu **Translation** / *Traduction* : Jane Mitchell, Maryse Désaulniers, Sarah Duschesne-Fisette, Tina Sarazin and/*et* Julie Turbide **Editing (French)** / *Révision (français)* : Marie-Pierre Lavoie **Proofreading (French)** / *Lecture d'épreuves (français)* : Marie-Pierre Lavoie and/*et* Tina Sarazin

Project and photography management / *Gestion de projet et de photographie* : Julie Morgan **Project management** / *Gestion de projet* : Alison Maclean and/*et* Monica Netupsky **Planning management** / *Gestion de la planification* : Lise Carrière

Special thanks to / *Nous tenons également à remercier* : Len Apedaile · Ellen Babers · Greg Bartels · Derek Baxter · Ryan Bennetts · Janet Bernat · Myriam Berry · Jennifer Boucher · Anthony Bocquetin · Paul Brosseau · Karen Bryan · Jessica Burton · Alastair Cameron · Katharine Carol · Daren Clark · Dave Cobb · Carmen Coccimiglio · Amanda Cohen · Sam Corea · Stephanie Cornish · Tom Cornwall · Robert Cousin · Slobodan Delic · Stephane Delisle · Hilary Dunn · Madeline Ell · Rick Etkin · Eric Fremont · Logan Frison · Kristin Fung · John Furlong · Katrina Galas · Chris Gear · Byron Go · Kim Gordon · Joanna Gould · Roberto Grassi · Mark Halliday · Tara Hatch · Elizabeth Hindle · Kevin Hodder · Vanessa Hodge · Bryce Holbech · Craig Holland · Russ Horner · Charles Hotel · Adrian Huang · Andrée Janyk · Nadine Jarry · Jordan Kallman · Dennis Kim · Mélanie Kimmett · Salman Manki · Marnie King · Elia Kriketos · Virginie Lamarche · Michelle Landry · Steve Lange · Krista Leesment · Craig Lehto · Candice Leung · Peta Lewis · Caroline Lotter · Sheryl MacDonald · Greg Magirescu · Michele Mamacos · Janey Marks · Kim Mathoney · Anne McDougall · Kate McLellan · Janet Miller · Jacqueline Moffatt · Kristina Molloy · Tina Morabi · Dave Newson · Tara Novak · Lisa Oakley · Patrick Okens · Carla Olson · Janeen Owen · Janine Palatin · Jane Park · Shawn Parkinson · Cino Picillo · Christiaan Piller · Karen Planden-Jeffery · Michelle Plotkin · Ian Pool · Cory Ransom · Ashley Roberts · Talia Rosales · Robin Russell · Max Saenger · Luca Santaniello · Nejat Sarp · Gail Seay · Pam Skeans · Eric Smith · Jennifer Smith · Cayla Spiess · Elaina Spring · Stewart Stolarski · Amanda Streams · Terry Summerton · Jennifer Sutherland · Chip Suttles · Tomo Tanaka · Michelle To · Elizabeth Urbach · Catriana van Rijn · Bev Viger · Glen Westrup · Jean Whitaker · Dene Wilson · Eileen Wong · Mark Woo · Vince Yu, and others who helped with this book in countless ways. / *ainsi que toutes les autres personnes qui ont participé de maintes façons à l'élaboration de ce livre.*

Online Public Comments / *Commentaires en ligne du public*

Best efforts have been made to ensure the accuracy of information in this book. / *On a déployé tous les efforts pour assurer l'exactitude des renseignements contenus dans ce livre.*

Library and Archives Canada Cataloguing in Publication

With Glowing Hearts: The Official Commemorative Book of the XXI Olympic Winter Games and the X Paralympic Winter Games / VANOC. Des plus brillants exploits : Le livre commémoratif officiel des XXI es Jeux olympiques d'hiver et des X es Jeux paralympiques d'hiver / COVAN.

Text in English and French.
ISBN 978-0-470-73618-0

1. Winter Olympic Games (21st : 2010 : Vancouver, BC).
2. Paralympic Winter Games (10th : 2010 : Vancouver, BC).
I. Vancouver Organizing Committee for the 2010 Olympic and Paralympic Winter Games II. Title: Des plus brillants exploits.

GV842.2010W48 2010   796.98
C2010-901526-6E

Catalogage avant publication de Bibliothèque et Archives Canada

With Glowing Hearts: The Official Commemorative Book of the XXI Olympic Winter Games and the X Paralympic Winter Games / VANOC. Des plus brillants exploits : Le livre commémoratif officiel des XXI es Jeux olympiques d'hiver et des X es Jeux paralympiques d'hiver / COVAN.

Texte en anglais et en français.
ISBN 978-0-470-73618-0

1. Jeux olympiques d'hiver (21 es : 2010 : Vancouver, C.-B.).
2. Jeux paralympiques d'hiver (10 es : 2010 : Vancouver, C.-B.).
I. Comité d'organisation des Jeux olympiques et paralympiques d'hiver de 2010 à Vancouver II. Titre : Des plus brillants exploits.

GV842.2010W48 2010   796.98
C2010-901526-6F

John Wiley & Sons Canada, Ltd.
6045 Freemont Blvd.
Mississauga, Ontario
L5R 4J3

Printed in Canada
Imprimé au Canada

1 2 3 4 5 FP 14 13 12 11 10

Mixed Sources
Cert no. SW-COC-001271
© 1996 FSC
FSC

WILEY

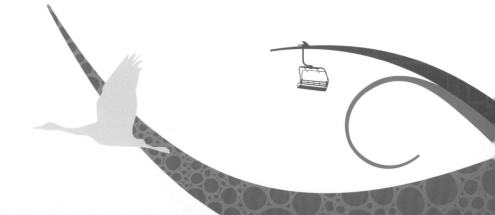